The Essence of
PARENTING

The Essence of
PARENTING

Anne Johnson and Vic Goodman

CROSSROAD • NEW YORK

1995

The Crossroad Publishing Company
370 Lexington Avenue, New York, NY 10017

Printed in the United States of America

Library of Congress Cataloging-in-Publication Data

Johnson, Anne (Anne M.) 1959–
   The essence of parenting / Anne Johnson and Vic Goodman.
      p.   cm.
   ISBN 0-8245-1507-2 (pbk.)
   1. Parenting.   I. Goodman, Vic, 1948–   . II. Title.
HQ755.8.J64   1995
649'.1–dc20   95-13754
                                                                CIP

To Scott and Lorelle,

Hannah, Claire, Martha, Emily, and Jenny —

for all you've had to put up with the past two years.

This book is for you with all our love and gratitude.

Contents

We hope the *The Essence of Parenting* will point the way to a deeper understanding of what inhibits our ability to live and parent spontaneously from the heart. Parenting is a living process filled with infinite possibilities. It is not static, where we learn something once and then never have to change our approach or our perspective. It is about each of us finding *our own* right way, a way filled with love and joy and peace of mind.

This book is offered as a guide or simply as food for thought. It is not meant as the gospel according to Anne and Vic. So if from time to time we sound too opinionated, ignore us.

Introduction

Wanting to be the best parent possible is a worthy ideal. For many of us, it has been the driving force in our lives ever since we made the decision or at least accepted the responsibility of being a parent. One mom expressed it beautifully in a letter to us: "When my son was born I remember holding him in my arms and vowing to be such a good mother that he would hardly ever need to cry. I actually thought that if I was a good enough mother my child would never be unhappy."

Over the years of teaching, counseling, and writing we have known many people who have made similar vows, ourselves included. So many of us struggle to do our best, exhausting ourselves emotionally, physically, and spiritually in the attempt to create a utopian life for ourselves and our children. Guilt, disappointment, and frustration plague us when what we experience falls short of our ideal.

Equipped with determination and the best of intentions, there are those of us who refuse to give up our quest. Hoping to find the secret, the magic formula that will turn our *longing* for harmony and happiness in our role as parents into *reality*, we turn to devouring every parenting book ever written. Some books are bought and never even opened. Just having them on our shelves makes us feel better. Their presence provides comfort and reassurance that it *is* possible to do parenting right, to capture the optimal experience we just have to read a few more hundred pages and we'll have the situation under control.

What so many of us eventually wake up to discover is that intellectual understanding can take us only so far — and, in fact, may itself become an obstacle in achieving the experience

13

we covet. What we truly long for is contentment and joy. What we want more than anything for our children is that they too experience the love and joy, the contentment and satisfaction of all life has to offer. This experience we want so desperately, which feels so elusive and unattainable through reading books, is the experience of living from the heart.

Once we are awakened to this truth, that what we seek lies within our own heart, not within the pages of a book or in the creation of some perfect external situation, we soon discover another truth: we can give only that which we already possess. The one true gift, the only gift of lasting value we can pass on to our children is our own inner state.

Until we learn to live from the heart, what we hope to give our children will always be out of reach. If we live our lives filled with doubt, plagued with anxiety, guilt, worry, fear, anger, judgment, or criticism, this is what our children will inherit. If we live our lives with a feeling of self-acceptance, gratitude, honesty, and trust we pass on an entirely different legacy.

Why is it so hard at times to live from the heart, to feel love, to be able to relax and enjoy being a parent? *Fear.* Fear of anger, fear of losing control, fear of what others will think of us, fear of doing it wrong and ruining our children, fear of failure. Somewhere along the way we all fall prey to fear — the controlling state of mind that thinks and doubts, worries and withholds, blames and projects. Once we are able to leave our fears by the roadside, we can travel the journey of parenthood with joy.

Without fear, doing parenting "right" ceases to be an issue. Without fear, parenting becomes a joyful, spontaneous expression of our uniqueness as a human being. All it takes is a willingness to be ourselves, to listen to ourselves, to trust ourselves.

If we can accomplish this much in our role as parents, to honestly know and be ourselves, then all we have to do is be available and our children will find the love and nourishment they need. The more we are able to live our lives in a simple and straightforward manner, guided by the innate wisdom and love of the human heart, the more support and nourishment our children will receive. It happens as naturally as the sun giving light.

This is not to say life will suddenly become rosy and be without its trials; we are, after all, human beings. We will always feel the full range of human emotions and experience the full range of human reactions. The issue is more what we do with them when we have them. Once we are no longer caught in the grip of fear, we will be free to embrace the rich diversity of what being a parent has to offer — the ups and downs, the joys and sorrows, the harmony and chaos — without losing heart, without feeling overwhelmed, without wondering why we ever had children in the first place.

If we are willing, we can learn to see and accept everything as part of the play of life, as lessons to be learned, as limitations to overcome. We can teach ourselves to live without worry and without judgment, to enter into the play of parenting — of life — with an open heart and a steady mind. Yet before we can taste the full sweetness of life, we must stop being afraid. In order to feel the love and joy we long for, that we felt so readily when our children were born, we must first learn to find it within ourselves.

How do we eliminate fear? How do we reach the love and joy, the harmony and contentment we are seeking and want so much for our children? By choosing to become conscious. By learning to recognize all of the thoughts and feelings that shape our moods, our attitudes, our behaviors, that color our experience of life, and by choosing to not be influenced by them. By realizing that love and joy are not dependent on circumstances outside of ourselves or people acting a certain way, that love and joy already exist within the heart.

Once we are grounded in our own inner love there will be no room for fear. Once we are grounded in our inner love, we can stop the endless chase for answers outside of ourselves. All we need to know will be revealed to us. To reach the love, to find and stay connected to the heart, does require effort on our part;

yet effort alone will not reveal the hidden treasure. To become established in love requires the combination of grace and self-effort. Becoming conscious, being willing to make the effort, opening ourselves to grace — these are the keys that unlock the heart.

Like a homing beacon, the heart calls us home: the love, the joy, the wisdom are alive within us. It is there we must find them. The foundation of parenting, the true essence of parenting, is an open heart and a steady mind. The heart truly does know the way.

The Essence of Parenting began as lessons in a correspondence course. We wrote them for ordinary people reaching for the highest, yearning for the optimal experience parenting has to offer. We wrote them for ourselves. They evolved out of a living process with people who were ready to become conscious about their parenting, people who were ready to learn to trust the wisdom of the heart. As you read you will hear their questions, feel their concerns; undoubtedly their words will echo your own thoughts and experiences.

The book format came into being simply because we wanted to reach more people, to offer comfort and hope, to point the way back to the heart for those who had become lost in their search for love as the foundation of parenting.

We urge you to read this book slowly. Read no more than one chapter a week or two chapters a month. Reread each chapter as often as you can. Take the time to contemplate what you have read. Ask yourself the questions and listen patiently for the answers. See if what you've read has meaning in your life.

A great teacher once said: "It is not a matter of how many new things we can learn, as much as it is how many times we can learn what we think we already know." One important aspect of this book is that the more often you read the chapters and consistently put into practice what is being offered, the more growth you will experience in your life.

The Essence of Parenting will consistently encourage you to shift your focus from external circumstances and relationships to the space where everything originates and where everything is understood: the heart. You already know this space. It is the silent witness: that nonjudgmental, noncritical, nonevaluating observer who has witnessed every thought, every emotion, and every event that has ever taken place in your life. This space of the heart is the same in each of us, and it is in this space that we will meet each time you pick up the book.

By choosing to read *The Essence of Parenting* you are embarking on a journey that can change not only your view of parenting, but your life as well. It is a journey that is both exhilarating and demanding, a journey that requires effort, yet happens as much by grace. It is a journey that will lead to *conscious* rather than unconscious parenting and living. By choosing to participate, you are making a commitment to choose positive, healthy, and loving responses to situations in your life. You are choosing to trust the wisdom of the heart.

Chapter One

If we are not aware of this basic truth, that love is our inner essence, our natural inner state, then everything else we think we know or attempt to do will not bring about the contentment or harmony we are seeking in our life.

Haven't you found it amazing at times that an intelligent, well-informed, and well-intentioned person like yourself could end up losing it so often with your kids? We know we have. Parenting looked so easy; it seemed like it would be fun and a fairly simple task to master, that it would be easy not to repeat all the mistakes our parents made.... Were we deluded! What happened anyway? Did we miss something somewhere? How did we end up feeling so unsure of ourselves, questioning every move we make with our kids?

It's been our experience that the majority of people struggling with the challenges of parenthood are dumbfounded first and foremost by the responsibility of disciplining their children. When our babies turn into kids, we're suddenly faced with the job of guiding them into being socially acceptable and appropriate, not to mention making them tolerable to live with at home. We try what we logically think will work in the discipline department, and it backfires. We try something else that we read about or heard about on a talk show and it takes us only so far. We worry about being too strict or too lenient, about damaging our children's self-esteem and at the same time have a sinking feeling that our own is going down the drain. We can't believe it when we find ourselves yelling and (heaven forbid) spanking our kids when we swore we would never resort to such tactics.

We keep looking for the answers. We're all too familiar with the questions. Is there a way to do this in a natural and loving way that works? What am I doing wrong? What's wrong with my kids? What's wrong with me?

Up until now, the answers you've found to these questions in books or from experts on the speaking circuit may have looked like lists of techniques or "how-tos." They may have appeared as diagnostic tools to help you figure out just what your problem is or what's wrong with you or your children so that you can then apply the correct solution. Some suggestions you've come upon may have been very helpful and comforting; others may have left you puzzled and discouraged. Regardless, the fact that you are reading yet *another* book indicates that something in you has yet to be satisfied.

We hope that the days of being haunted by nagging doubts will soon be behind you. Desperation will diminish. It should be only a matter of time before you are able to rest assured that there is not some crucial piece of information out there that you are missing but that could turn your parenting abilities around overnight — a piece of information buried in still another text on parenting that reads like a car manual. "If Part C on Diagram F-1 isn't working properly try Solution S6 on page 360." Or in parenting lingo, "If your child does such and such, or fits into this or that category, implement X,Y, and Z and your problems will be over."

We are not implying that you will never again refer to books with helpful suggestions on understanding your children developmentally. Or that you will never pick up a book that offers insight into important issues related to child-rearing or offers practical ideas about healthy parenting skills.

But we hope that you will lay aside and never again pick up your belief that anything is going wrong, that there is something that has to be fixed. These beliefs are the very thoughts that fuel our fears and self-doubts and keep us on the frenzied chase in search of answers from outside of ourselves. A chase not unlike a dog after its own tail.

You won't find any prescriptions for what ails you or your children in this book. As we have already said, and will remind you of again and again, there is nothing to fix. Nothing is broken. The time has come to take our focus off whatever we think isn't working in our lives and to begin looking within ourselves to find the origin of whatever *we think* is going wrong.

It's time to begin peeling away the layers of false beliefs and denial that keep us barking up the wrong tree. Trying to fix or change anything outside of ourselves without first turning our attention within is like trying to change the way we look by fixing the reflection in the mirror.

Everything happens within. Once we connect to our true inner state, love, our external circumstances will be a natural reflection of that love. This concept may sound foreign, and even unbelievable to you right now. But over time you will *experience* it to be true; you won't have to take our word for it.

Let's begin to work out of this new perspective — that everything happens within — by applying it to that pressing problem most parents are perplexed by: discipline. You think you have to figure out how to discipline your children? Guess again. Consider instead turning the question around to yourself. Remember, there is nothing *out there* for you to fix. But if you take a moment to look within, you might discover that *you* are the one in need of discipline. A scary thought!

Before we can become effective disciplinarians we need to learn how to discipline ourselves. Why? Because discipline is a necessary ingredient in our lives for maximum health, happiness, and ultimate freedom. When we lead disciplined lives, we set beautiful examples for our children.

Does it feel as if you don't have the energy or desire to be self-disciplined? Do you find yourself resisting the notion of having more discipline in your life? Some of the negative feelings you may be having probably come from misunderstanding the word "discipline." On the basis of our past experiences, many of us have come to equate the word "discipline" with the word "punishment." Who in their right mind would want to bring more self-inflicted punishment into their lives?

Interestingly, the two words are not the least bit related to each other. The definition of "punishment" is "to cause a person to undergo pain, loss, or suffering for a crime or wrong-doing." The definition of "discipline" is "training that develops self-control, character, or orderliness" (Webster). If we are doing a good job of disciplining ourselves and our children we will rarely, if ever, need to punish ourselves or our children. In fact, as we become more self-disciplined we may become aware of areas in our life where we have been unknowingly punishing ourselves. Replacing punishment with discipline will feel like a luxury. Does this seem far-fetched? Read on.

Think of the times we most often resort to punishing our kids — threatening, yelling, hitting. If we're honest, most of us will have to admit that lack of alternatives isn't the problem. Consistently putting those alternatives into practice is. Why is that? Could it really be that we are a bit remiss in self-discipline?

As I have learned to stand back and witness my reactions to my children, I have noticed that I resort to punishment when I feel afraid or out of control or simply worn out. Whenever I balance the checkbook, am faced with an overly messy house, or am preoccupied with a stressful situation at work, I have the tendency to snap more quickly at the kids. Subconsciously, I'm letting my fears get the upper hand. As a result, I take control where and how I can, a natural reaction to fear and weariness — by yelling at someone smaller than me.

If I'm lucky, I get immediate results and maybe some brief, fleeting satisfaction. I blow off some steam and feel a little bit more in control again. The problem is that, I am doing all this at my children's expense. Besides setting a poor example, I'm using my children as a depository for my negative emotions, possibly hurting their self-esteem and doing damage to our relationship.

In addition to all this, I end up feeling guilty more often than not; the bills still aren't paid; the house is still a mess; the situation at the office remains unchanged. Where has punishment gotten me? And who is being punished? If I never stood back and questioned the scenario, I'd probably still be doing it regularly. What's more, I'd probably be justifying my reactions by saying I was "disciplining" my children. Sound familiar?

Having practical parenting strategies available to replace yelling does help. But in all fairness, I must admit that I had probably read every book available on alternatives and still I found myself resorting to that age-old tactic of yelling at the top of my lungs. But it's not the number of positive techniques we have in our arsenal that determines the way we experience and react to a situation; it's our emotional state. And more than anything, our emotional state is determined by our level of self-discipline.

Let's face it, we're going to have negative thoughts, feelings, and reactions because we're human; that's not the problem. Being self-disciplined does not mean repressing or denying our feelings. Self-discipline means looking at where our thoughts, feeling, and reactions are coming from and at what we do with them once they appear on the scene. What set me up to explode? What thoughts and fears about not having enough money, not getting all the work done, not living up to expectations at work started the pot boiling? What angry feelings toward my spouse or co-worker were lurking just beneath the surface? What beliefs led me to skip lunch, take on a tedious task when I was already tired, and not take a well-deserved rest or break? Wasn't I punishing myself with all my negative thinking and then projecting my feelings of worry and inadequacy onto my children in the form of blame and scolding? Was it really something my kids did that deserved all that wrath? Would I have responded differently if I was in a different frame of mind and body?

By taking the time to question why we act the way we do, or why certain feelings keep coming up in certain situations, we may be able to prevent a lot of unwanted, unnecessary behavior in both ourselves and our children. But it takes discipline to slow down and do self-inquiry. It takes effort. It takes a willingness to be open and to change our perspective. That's what this book is all about.

This might feel overwhelming, especially if we have never before taken the time to pay attention to what our everyday thoughts, feelings, and reactions are telling us. Yet it is possible if we take it slowly and one step at a time begin to be disciplined about practicing self-inquiry. Disciplined self-inquiry requires patience and persistence; it necessitates dropping our self-judgments so shame and fear can't keep us from looking objectively at what is going on. This process of becoming the witness of our thoughts is what will help us gain access to our inner love. It will help us clear away all the thoughts, feelings, and beliefs that keep us from experiencing our true inner state, the foundation for healthy discipline: love.

One of the first questions we can ask ourselves as we begin to reevaluate our need for more self-discipline is one we referred to earlier. Just what is our understanding and perception of the concept of discipline? Are we confusing discipline with punishment? Do we need to examine our assumptions and preconceived ideas in order to openly embrace this important ingredient in our life?

Consider this: the root word of "discipline" is "disciple." Take a moment to reflect on any of the great master/disciple relationships you have been exposed to in literature or religion over the course of your life. True masters as well as authentic disciples base their relationships with one another on love, respect, and devotion. True masters practice what they preach, they serve as much as they are served, they are the embodiment of the lessons they strive to impart to their students.

Isn't this the type of relationship we hope to have with our children — to be not only a teacher but a loving example they will spontaneously wish to follow? Love is the foundation of the teacher; love is what makes the student want to learn; love is what inspires spontaneous feelings of devotion. Finding our own inner love and immersing ourselves in it will make it possible to discipline ourselves and our children more effectively.

Why? Because love motivates from within while punishment teaches children to monitor their behavior on the basis of fear of a force outside of themselves. Fear bred by punishment is eventually disabling. Fear leads to resentment, contempt, isolation, shame, and guilt. Children who learn to comply through punishment are dependent on an outside agent of control to monitor their behavior. Remove the authority figure and what is left to motivate behavior — the above-mentioned by-products of fear. Is this what we want for our children?

Love, by comparison, fosters confidence, respect, and gratitude. When children are disciplined out of love they become established in these virtues that remain intrinsically a part of their character. They become governed by an internalized sense of right and wrong, a moral code rooted in love and respect. Isn't this the ultimate goal of disciplining our children, that they mature into self-governed individuals possessing a strong foundation of love and respect?

Take a few moments and reflect on how strongly love permeates your life. How often is love the foundation of what you do or a motivating factor for your behavior? When you finish reading this paragraph, put the book down; close your eyes; let yourself become still. See if in the quiet you are able to feel the love we've been talking about.

If you have trouble finding and feeling love, you're not alone. Many of us have become so busy and out of touch with the feeling it seems not to exist. Some of you might be wondering if it was ever there in the first place. Don't worry; it hasn't gone anywhere. The love we're talking about is our natural inner state. We were born with it. Once we are able to reconnect with it — more precisely, with ourselves — we will be able to share this love with everyone, even people we don't like.

We are not talking about an unreachable ideal. We are talking about the underlying foundation of true humanity. If we are not aware of this basic truth, that love is our inner essence, our natural inner state, then everything else we think we know or attempt to do will not bring about the contentment or harmony we are seeking in our life.

So what happened when you closed your eyes? Did your mind run wild? Perhaps it is in need of a little discipline. No need to worry: over the course of time, as you read and understand more, your mind will find the discipline it needs. The mind, by the way, is *not* the silent witness — that nonjudgmental, noncritical, nonevaluating observer — we referred to in the introduction. The mind, as you probably already know, is way too busy thinking to notice anything.

Take a few moments and close your eyes again. Find the natural rhythm of your breath and let yourself relax. Consider your life as you are living it now. Are there any areas that feel out of balance and could use more self-discipline? Remember, we're talking about discipline, not punishment. For example, do you offer yourself enough time to rest? Do you eat nutritious food at a relaxed pace? Do you play often and get regular exercise? Do you manage adult time away from your children? Do you enjoy sex and have a sex life that meets your needs? Are there excesses in your eating, drinking, or spending habits?

Recognize the areas in your life that could use more loving discipline. This is not a time to criticize or judge yourself for being out of balance; we all are to some degree, so relax. There is no need to feel shame or belittle yourself for not being perfect. Becoming conscious is the precursor to change and growth. Keep breathing. Make a commitment to offer yourself the love, time, and patience needed to gradually make any changes that will bring about greater balance for you and your family. This is the essence of self-discipline. And isn't it encouraging to know that *this* is what you are going to offer yourself in greater proportions over the course of time?

In these quiet moments of introspection, you may also find it useful to reflect upon the people in your life who were or still are inspiring teachers. Think about the love and admiration they have inspired in you. Let yourself be nourished by this love for as long as you can. Did you know that this love can actually begin to transform your life if you just take the time to *remember* that it is there underneath your habitual thoughts and feelings? It's that easy; even though you'll be amazed at how often you forget to remember.

Rereading this chapter several times before going on to the next may help you remember the truth about love being your inner essence, the foundation of self-discipline. It takes a certain amount of discipline to reread something you think you already know. Try it anyway. It may serve as an opportunity to practice bringing self-discipline into your life.

This week observe whether your typical responses are based in love or in fear. See if you can shift your emphasis to love. It will help to slow down, breathe deeply, and remember that at your essence *you are love*. With a feeling of love, teach your children what is expected of them by example, rather than by threatening, manipulating, or trying to control them with force.

And if you experience difficulty making the shift, keep trying; it takes practice, practice, practice. Maybe you're tired, overworked, overscheduled, underfed, or overspent. Remember, responding to our own basic needs with love and compassion is really the first step in becoming self-disciplined; and self-discipline is what will make us effective disciplinarians.

Notice how your emotional state affects your children and your perception of what is happening. Try to catch yourself when you're disciplining out of fear. In reality, you won't be disciplining if it's out of fear; you'll be punishing. Anger, a feeling we're all very familiar with as parents, is often motivated by fear. Practice self-inquiry. If you're angry, are you also afraid? What is simmering in your pot that needs your attention? Have you been punishing yourself instead of loving yourself? Whatever the case, try to remember that your feelings are what will determine the way you experience any situation and not the other way around.

In time we will begin to see that whatever we want for our children we must first experience in our own life. So it always makes sense to look within rather than trying to control others or the situation. When our inner state comes into balance through the process of self-discipline, choosing positive parenting techniques will become all but effortless. Without self-discipline, we will most likely spend our time and energy trying to change or mold our children into the image of what we want them to be — often a reflection of what is missing in our own life. Coming into harmony with our life is the best way to lead our children into satisfaction with theirs.

Chapter Two

*It is very hard to be responsive to others when we are being
unresponsive to ourselves.*

Some people find it hard to believe that love is their natural
inner state. I know I did. When my sister first suggested that
deep in my heart was an ocean of love, I didn't believe her.
I was sure that although this might be true for everyone else
in the world, it couldn't possibly be true for me. I was afraid
that if I were to close my eyes and look inside, all I would find
would be anger and fear.

How did you do closing your eyes and looking inside for
love? Some of us find it difficult to sit with our eyes closed.
As soon as we try it seems as if our minds become hyper-
active: grocery lists, dinner plans, projects at work, phone calls
to make, places to go, people we're mad at. Some of us are so
used to rushing through our day trying to get everything done
that it seems unnatural to sit quietly for a few moments. Nor-
mally we are so focused on doing for others that taking a few
minutes to reflect on our own life, let alone our inner state, may
seem like a waste of our time.

Reading this book will serve as a reminder to slow down
and pay attention to yourself. Even if you are not sure why
you are being asked to do this or what the benefits will be,
try it anyway. Taking time to breathe and reflect on your inner
state will over time help to expand your understanding as well
as your ordinary state of consciousness. Remember one of the
main goals in reading this book is to learn how to parent and
live consciously — fully aware and with an open heart. This

doesn't happen by magic or by willing it to be so. It requires self-discipline.

What have you noticed about your predominant feelings lately? Have you taken time to consider what is out of balance in your life and what your needs are? You haven't? Take a few minutes; we'll wait for you.

Neediness is one of the primary causes of disharmony. Yet once we understand our own needs and start taking care of them, everything will start to feel better. Taking care of our needs not only makes us feel better; it helps us become more sensitive to our children.

Conversely, not understanding our own needs will make it difficult to accept and respond lovingly to our children's needs. If we find it difficult to take care of ourselves — in other words, we're not living a healthy, balanced life — how can we have this expectation for our kids? We must live our own lives as the example we wish to have followed. Not to live this way subtly places an expectation on our children to be something we are not, and it will, without fail, erode our credibility. "Do as I say, not as I do" just doesn't cut it.

One of the biggest obstacles to overcome on the road to conscious parenting is not understanding our children's needs and how they affect behavior. To further complicate the matter, their needs keep changing as they grow and develop. If we knew what to expect and when to expect it, we would undoubtedly feel less frustrated and disillusioned and more in control. At the very least, we'd probably feel less inclined to ship our kids off or trade them in every time things get hairy. So much of our frustration and disappointment comes from not understanding our children's needs and, consequently, age-appropriate behavior.

Most of our parents had no idea what children needed emotionally. A conversation with my mother revealed that her only source of information on how to parent was a book written by Dr. Benjamin Spock, a well-known pediatrician. According to my mother, if it wasn't in Dr. Spock's book, she didn't know about it. Child psychology wasn't even an established field of study until the 1940s. Obviously there is much more information available to us now than there was to our parents. Consequently, it's not fair to fault our parents for not always knowing what they were doing; they really didn't know. We, however, have fewer excuses.

With a little conscious effort we can come to understand our own needs as well as our children's needs. One thing is certain: using our newfound awareness to make positive changes in *our* life will positively affect everyone else in our family. Why? Because when we're happy, our kids are happy. When we're relaxed, our kids are more relaxed. When all's right with us, all's right with the world.

Take a few minutes and reflect on what you've read up to this point. Are you having to adjust your thinking to accommodate what we are suggesting? Are you wondering what planet we're from? Simply notice what's going on inside. Become aware of what you are feeling: agitated, defensive, impatient, accepting, joyful? maybe relieved? Since there is no right or wrong way to be feeling, just take notice and allow the feelings to be there.

Now that you're in a heightened state of awareness — it only takes a slight shift in your attention — let's do an exercise that may just open your eyes. First, get a pencil and paper. When you finish reading the paragraph, close your eyes. Take a few deep breaths, and let yourself relax. Let yourself become still for a few minutes. Now imagine a child in his or her most beautiful state — you know, the kind of kid they put on Kodak commercials or in Hershey chocolate ads; or maybe envision your own child asleep in all her innocence. As you think about that child, create a list of all the qualities that little one embodies, and write them down under the heading "Childlike."

When you've come up with a fairly long list, close your eyes again and imagine a child at his worst. For example, picture your own child on those days when things are so bad you curse the day you met your spouse. Make a second list and place all the qualities that describe this type of child under the heading "Childish."

Now look at the two lists you've just created. Can you guess what underlying factor determines which list best describes a child on a given day? Most likely, childlike children are having their needs met, while childish children are not.

Here's another way to interpret the lists. Think of your typical approach with your child. Does it resemble the first list or the second? When we are self-disciplined disciplinarians, that is, parents who take conscious and consistent responsibility for taking care of ourselves and getting our needs met, we respond from our childlike self. When we are needy from lack of self-discipline, our mind, emotions, and habits run wild and we are prone to parent from our childish self. Be honest with yourself: which column looks like you most of the time? If you're not sure, ask someone else in your family.

Incidentally, childlike qualities are not a figment of our imagination. In fact, these qualities come close to describing our actual or true self or how we'd be most of the time if we took care of ourselves. Amazing isn't it? Meeting or not meeting everyone's needs in healthy ways is what determines the emotional climate of our households. Can you see why it is so important to understand what our needs and our children's needs are and how to best meet them?

If you found it hard to come up with your own lists, we've included ours at the end of the chapter. If you catch yourself acting like the childish list, ask yourself what you might be needing. When you notice that you are immersed in a childlike state, be aware of what you are doing that is healthy and loving for yourself and keep right on doing it.

When my kids were very small I was stressed-out a lot. At one time, all three of my children were under four years of age. I was working outside the home and also trying to be a super housekeeper, wife, and volunteer at church and school. I was a walking "Child*ish*" list. I crabbed and whined and lost my temper more times than not. I honestly felt it was my right to be a grouch. After all, look at everything I did for everyone. What a martyr! And everyone was so ungrateful. No one could blame me for losing it: I deserved to!

Over time, however, this approach just didn't make sense. Maybe I had a right to my feelings, but did I really have the right to unload them all on my family? And what good was it doing me to hold on to all that negative emotion day after day, even if I had the right to feel that way? I was like a squirrel storing away resentment after resentment. I would keep score of all I did for everybody else — supposedly because I liked helping people — and yet it seemed like I never got paid back. I was in the habit of giving my spouse a litany at the end of the day of everything that had gone wrong. No wonder I felt depressed and angry all the time. No wonder I felt justified having tantrums. If someone had told me that at my essence I was love, I would have popped that person in the nose.

Slowly I began to awaken to the fact that what I had the right to was to be aware of my feelings. Along with that right, I had the responsibility to do what was needed to get them back into balance or, better yet, to prevent them from becoming out of balance. If I was short-tempered, was it because I had skipped lunch or because I stayed up too late cleaning the house before going to bed? Had I overextended myself helping others to win their praise and keep up my image?

What I had a right to was this: when I first noticed I was hungry, I had the right to eat something healthy in a relaxed fashion. When I felt tired I had the right to hit the sack and let the house be a mess for at least eight more hours. I had the right to say no to the request to be in charge of the school rummage sale so I would have time to play during the week. I had the right to slow down and pay attention to my feelings so I could recognize my needs.

For obvious reasons, it's easier to notice our extreme emotions like frustration, rage, disgust, or self-hate than it is to notice the more subtle ones. We must begin to recognize extreme reactions in our life as red flags: warnings that an important internal cue was missed earlier that required a response. When we miss our chance to respond to our feelings, we've missed a chance to take care of a need. That's when we end up feeling on the edge and about to lose control. Subtle feelings deserve our attention, but we will have to slow down and shift our attention inside if we're going to notice them. Once we do, however, we can acknowledge them before things get out of hand. This doesn't happen by magic or by willing it to be so. It requires effort on our part; and effort requires self-discipline.

Because we have become so accustomed to focusing on what's going on around us rather than inside us, many of us don't know, or have forgotten, what our basic needs are. In the chapters ahead we will address the needs of children from infancy through adolescence and also learn practical, healthy ways to respond to them. At the same time, we'll track the needs common to all of us, becoming aware of those areas in our lives where we ignore, neglect, deny, or overindulge our needs — or our feelings. Why should we care? Because ignoring, denying, or neglecting our needs is what gradually transforms us from loving parents into ogres.

Walking through the stages of life and exploring needs can be an eye-opening experience that illustrates how alike we are. After all, we started from the same place and followed the same course of development; yet most of the time we're focused only on our differences. Consider for a minute who might be reading this book. Some are female; others are male. Some are married; others are single, divorced, or separated. Some live in blended families. Some have important, high-powered jobs; others live simple lives. Some have children who are little, while others have children who are practically adults. We may wear different clothes, eat different foods, and have varied political and religious beliefs, but there is one factor that undeniably binds us all together: we are human beings.

As you read this chapter, continue assessing your own needs

and see if you can determine what is missing in your life. Take time to reflect on how alike we are and how we all need and want basically the same things. Stop looking at differences and thinking that one way of being is more right than another. Remember to love and be gentle with yourself as you start to bring your life back into balance. Offer yourself whatever it is that you need. We think you will like what begins to happen as a result.

CHILDLIKE	CHILDISH
innocent	whiny
joyful	stubborn
cooperative	demanding
thoughtful	complaining
open	manipulative
serene	disrespectful
grateful	unappreciative
trusting	pushy
helpful	hurtful
sensitive	rude
spontaneous	know it all
enthusiastic	obnoxious
creative	uncooperative
gentle	selfish
generous	jealous
supportive	destructive
content	sarcastic
energetic	loud
considerate	hyperactive
polite	spiteful
angelic	hateful

Chapter Three

Much of our frustration and difficulty in parenting is a function of our own unresolved conflicts and emotions, not our children's behavior.

Can you remember back to when you first decided that you wanted a child? Some of us knew from the time we were little that we wanted to raise a family, while others of us were quite surprised to find ourselves in the family way. Having a child may have been the answer to prayers, an unwanted intrusion that we were unprepared for, or anything in between. What was it for you?

I was convinced that I didn't want any children. When Lorelle and I were in our early twenties and still quite idealistic and worried about the sorry state of the world, we were sure that adding more children to our planet's rapidly swelling population was not a good idea. Then one day in my late twenties I woke up, literally, knowing that I wanted to be a father. When I presented this to Lorelle I discovered that she had been thinking exactly the same thing about becoming a mother. Our idealism had given way to a powerful urge to reproduce.

Not everyone makes a conscious choice about becoming a parent. Over the years we've worked with many people who experienced dramatic changes in their lives because of an unplanned or unwanted pregnancy. In some cases a pregnancy simply deepened an already existing relationship. The addition of a child, although unplanned, was accepted or even welcomed. In other cases, the prospect of becoming parents —

having to provide for and take care of a baby — was not so welcomed.

One young man I worked with several years ago was married and the father of a two-year-old son. He had been a sophomore in college planning on a career in graphic arts when his girlfriend informed him that she was pregnant. There was never a doubt in his mind about what he felt was the right thing for him to do. He and his girlfriend agreed to get married, and it was decided that he would drop out of school and find a job that would support their family.

He was not in love with his girlfriend at the time she became pregnant, and there had been no talk of getting married. His personal plans, overnight, became secondary. He was scared and angry about this turn of events and blamed his girlfriend — as well as himself — for their carelessness. His anger grew into bitterness and resentment and in time led to heavy drinking and acts of violence directed toward his wife.

Both he and his wife had accepted the fact that they were going to be parents and wanted to make a good home for their child. The problem was, emotionally he never reconciled the unplanned change of direction in his life. At the age of twenty-three he found himself living in conflict, torn by his desire to do the right thing. He loved his son and wanted to be a good father, but he resented the fact that this had not been his choice.

Another woman we know found herself in a completely different situation. Already the mother of a little boy, she knew that she wanted another baby. Unfortunately, her husband was not in agreement. In spite of this, the woman became pregnant and eventually delivered a beautiful, healthy baby girl. Her husband's support, however, from the moment of conception until delivery was nowhere to be seen; and several years after the birth their daughter it is still virtually nonexistent.

In a sense, it appeared as if this woman was being punished for having another child. Angry and resentful, her husband withheld not only his verbal and emotional support, but his affection as well. Sadly, she was not to be touched in a loving way by her husband for several years, bringing their sex life to a standstill. Instead of enjoying the love and companionship of her spouse, this mother found herself immersed in feelings of grief, loneliness, anger, and rejection. On top of everything, efforts to communicate her unhappiness were stalled by her husband's apparent disdain and her own longstanding difficulty in expressing herself.

Although they were the parents of two children, their marriage was no longer a partnership. Both the husband and wife were living their day-to-day lives feeling unhappy and emotionally distant, each blaming the other for their predicament. Their inability to resolve their emotional conflicts became a source of pain and disharmony in their lives, a wound that would not heal. Their children suffered with them.

Fortunate is the child who lands in the arms of adults who are content with their lives. Parents who are not preoccupied with their own worries or emotional conflicts are able to respond lovingly and spontaneously to their baby. Contented parents are free to gurgle back at their baby, notice its beauty and pureness of heart and revel in it. Their voices carry the energy of love, acceptance, and affirmation. Parents who are not weighted down with their own emotional turmoil are able to respond patiently to their child's needs. A child raised in such an environment will see his or her own natural inner Self mirrored back.

What a different experience a child has who arrives in a home where the parent's emotional state is typically anger, resentment, depression, agitation, fear, or worry. We know from early on our perception of ourselves and our world is heavily influenced by our parents' emotional state and their responses to us. We either learn to recognize and connect with our spontaneous self, love, seeing that reflected back to us, or we begin to develop a sense of identity by taking on our parents' feelings. Babies do not discriminate; they will absorb and internalize whatever they are exposed to.

Consider for a moment the implications of what you have read so far. What do we think has been predominantly mirrored back to your child? If you are preparing for the arrival of a child, whether newborn or not, what is the condition of your own emotional state at the present time? Think about how important it is to be free enough to recognize and respond to your child's innocence and purity of heart without being encumbered by your own unresolved emotions.

For some of us it may be painful to actually consider what is happening in our own life and how it affects our children. Maybe having a child was a strategy to repair or revitalize a failing marriage or relationship. Maybe having a child was a way to get back at someone we were angry with or perhaps a way to lift ourselves out of a depression and give our life meaning. Maybe having a child was simply a mistake! People have many reasons for having a child but often have not thought about how their life is going to affect that child — nor have they thought about how having a child is going to affect their life.

However it is that we ended up becoming a parent, we can take time to reflect on what we are currently offering our children. So much of our frustration and difficulty in parenting is a function of our own unresolved conflicts and emotions, not our children's behavior or flaws in their personality. This is not to suggest that our children are not responsible for their behavior; in fact, at times they can be an absolute pain in the neck (or back or posterior). We are merely pointing out that by recognizing our own feelings and understanding how they affect the people we live with, we can begin to create the intimacy we have been longing for in life. We *can* live consciously; and it does make a difference.

As we take time to think about how we are affecting our children, it's possible that memories will be triggered about our own early life experiences. Some of us might have happy memories, others may have painful memories, and still others will have no memories. There is no standard measure, no right or wrong experience to be having. Becoming conscious requires no self-judgment; it is only a matter of awareness. Seeing something about ourselves or our lives that has previously been repressed or unknown to us leads to greater freedom and spontaneity. It has been said that until we understand our own history we are doomed to repeat it.

Many people are unable to remember early childhood experiences. This does not necessarily imply that the memories were so painful they've been repressed. However, people who grew up in families where there was or still is active alcoholism, sexual abuse, violence, or some other powerfully debilitating influence or illness often have more than the usual difficulty remembering their past. It is not uncommon to block out painful or shame-filled memories; it is a built-in survival mechanism.

Parenting is probably the most demanding job we'll ever have and yet we have received little or no training for it. It is hard enough to parent effectively when we are the product of a healthy, happy family. It is virtually impossible to parent spontaneously and effectively when we are carrying around the emotional scars of a traumatic past. Whether consciously or unconsciously, we are a product of our upbringing.

Those of us who know or suspect that our family of origin has affected us in an adverse way might want to consider exploring this further in counseling. In the same way, those of us who know that our marriage or current relationship leaves us feeling empty and unsupported might also consider seeking help. Whether it's counseling, reading books, or talking to a friend or relative, help is available. And if it's any consolation, lots of people are dealing with the very same issues and feelings you are. You are not alone.

When you finish reading the next two paragraphs, close your eyes and let yourself relax. Gently bring your attention to the natural rhythm of the breath as it moves in and out, in and out, in and out. If your mind starts to wander, gently bring it back to watching each inhalation and each exhalation. Now, take a moment to find your real Self, the silent witness, that part of you that never changes. Know that the thoughts and feelings you have every day are *not* you; they are transitory and fleeting, constantly changing like the clouds in the sky.

Continue to breathe quietly for a while with your eyes closed. Pay no attention to the thoughts and feelings that are begging to be noticed. Instead, see if you can find that magnificent underlying expansiveness that has animated your personality from the very beginning of your life. Try to be conscious these next few weeks of how accepting you can be of yourself and others. Be aware that acceptance feels expansive while nonacceptance feels contracted. Practice recognizing and dropping all judgments.

Notice what gets in the way of self-acceptance: anger? fear? resentment? the need to be in control? See if you can let go of whatever is it is that is stopping you by consciously taking the time to connect with your deeper Self, that natural, pure state we all experienced as babies. This deeper inner state has always been available to us. All we need to do to experience it is remember — remember that it is there, patiently waiting to shower us with unconditional love, acceptance, and affirmation.

Think about whether love, acceptance, and affirmation were available to you as a child and whether they are now available to your child. Remember, even if they weren't available to you then, they are available to you now — if not from outside yourself, then certainly from inside yourself. We are quite capable of giving ourselves whatever we *think* we need or want from others. The beauty of this is that once we can give it to ourselves, others will receive it from us without our having to do anything.

Chapter Four

Whatever we are experiencing mentally and emotionally in our life will be passed on to our children through touch. Our job is to offer gentle, loving touch that carries the expression of our love, commitment, and protection.

Have you noticed how often we make reference to feelings? It's hard not to. Emotions, or feelings, add spice and color to what would otherwise be a bland existence. Moreover, they are a natural and healthy part of our make-up and greatly enrich our lives. Feelings are a common ground for sharing ourselves with each other and as such are meant to be experienced — not repressed or denied.

In a very real sense, our emotions are intricately related to the body and often can be felt as actual physical sensations or "feelings." When we were small children, the types of sensory experiences available to us had a major impact on the development of our feelings. When we are adults, our emotions continue to be affected by the input of our senses.

Before we are old enough to have complicated emotions, let alone understand them, our world is nothing but one continual sensory extravaganza. Think about it. A baby's experience of the world comes from the touch of its parents' hands, the warmth of its body next to someone else, the taste of sweet milk, the sound of voices, the smell of a familiar, safe person, and so on.

The range of possible sense experiences a baby can have is limitless. Take sound for instance. In one home a baby might hear soft gentle voices, laughter, singing, honest emotional exchanges, and soothing silences. In another home where things are a bit more chaotic, a baby might hear shouting, the loud disconnected voices of television and radios, irritated commands, and strained silences. Most of us probably have a home somewhere in between, depending on what time of day or day of the week we are talking about.

Try listening inwardly for a few minutes and bring to mind the types of sounds you might hear on a typical day. Ordinarily we filter out so much of what we're exposed to that it might be interesting to take one day and pay close attention to everything we hear from the time we wake up until we go to bed. Did you know the quality and nature of the sounds we hear are affecting our inner state whether we are conscious of them or not? Imagine what they can do to a child whose senses are wide open.

Close your eyes, take a deep breath, and let yourself relax. Block out everything you can except your sense of smell. What do you notice? Have you ever noticed that some odors are so offensive you hold your breath when exposed to them, while others can be so intoxicating you just can't seem to get enough? What about the smells a child takes in? This is probably something we give little thought to, but consider the different inner experience a child would have smelling the fragrance of flowers or freshly mown grass compared to inhaling the scent of stale cigarette smoke. Smell has a subtle but powerful effect on our disposition and outlook.

Consider the impact of what we see on our inner state. Our eyes are continually at work absorbing images. We've already alluded to the fact that facial expressions and emotions underlying them have a dramatic effect on our children. Other visual stimuli affect our little ones as well. For instance, the overstimulus of shopping malls, the rapid movement of television, or the whirl of rushing traffic can all distract a baby from its natural inner contentment. We know it certainly has that effect on us. Think about the countless images, colors, and shapes that come into your field of vision every day. Which ones leave you feeling open and expanded? Which ones leave you feeling unsettled? What are these same images capable of doing to an infant, or a child of any age for that matter?

The quality of any sensory experience strongly affects an infant's perception of itself and the world and is the foundation for the *feeling* life of that child. Rich, pleasant sensory experiences give way to inner experiences that are colorful and diverse. Bland, inanimate, sharp experiences leave the terrain of one's inner life desolate. Being conscious of our environment and the choices we make can enrich not only our own life, but our child's as well.

The most significant sensory experience for an infant is touch. How a baby is touched will set the stage for its social, emotional, and sexual life. The messages we communicate through our touch will be embedded in the memory of our child's being. Whatever we are experiencing mentally and emotionally in our own life will be passed on to our children through touch. Our job is to offer gentle, loving touch that carries the expression of our love, commitment, and protection.

Babies need a tremendous amount of affectionate, nonsexual touch. A child surrounded by safe, nurturing touch develops a basic sense of trust in the world. She can then devote her energy and attention to investigating the world without feeling afraid. Her world will be experienced as basically good and kind. On the other hand, hurtful touch that is rough or abusive has a devastating effect, leaving a child to conclude that people can't be trusted, or worse yet, that there is something in them that deserves to be abused.

Positive, healthy touch is essential for optimal well-being. Whether in the form of hugs, gentle massages, or simply holding hands, touch stimulates the nervous system. It encourages the release of tension and stress and is even believed to have a beneficial effect on the immune system.

Of course, as with everything else, giving and receiving loving touch may be easier said than done. It can be extremely difficult if the touch we're used to has been painful, abusive, or starkly nonexistent in our life. It can also be difficult when there is an accumulation of fatigue, resentment, anger, or fear standing as an insurmountable wall between us and our loved ones. If this happens to be true for you, take a deep breath and let yourself sigh. Over time, it is possible for this wall to gradually dissolve — if we want it to. In fact, it may just suddenly tumble down completely as we turn our attention inside and learn how to open our hearts.

Why waste any time? Stop right now. Put the book down and simply breathe. Let your thoughts go. Let the tension in your body melt away by directing your breath to any part of you that feels tense or agitated. Pay no attention to the myriad thoughts that seem to hang on and persist in spite of your efforts to ignore them. Be gentle with yourself and keep bringing your attention back to your breath. When you start to feel relaxed, drink in the splendor of that restful state for as long as you can. If you find you like the feeling, do it often: in the car while you're driving, while you're walking, lying in bed before you fall asleep. You won't miss any important thoughts; they'll be there waiting for you as soon as you're done relaxing.

Take time this week to notice if nurturing touch is missing from your relationships with your children. No matter what the age of a child, it's wonderful to bring more affectionate touch into his or her life. If your child is still an infant there are the basics: hold, rock, snuggle, massage. Teach other siblings loving ways to touch respectfully, like gentle patting on the baby's tummy or toes, blowing softly on his head, or stroking her cheek. Slow down and take time to sit and gaze into your baby's eyes rather than run that one extra errand. Sit in wonderment, and let your heart fill with love and gratitude at having the opportunity to share your life with this precious little being.

With older children, an arm around the shoulder while talking, a stroke on the cheek in greeting, holding hands while walking, a pat on the head at an unsuspecting moment, and back rubs or foot rubs before bed are all gentle and affectionate ways to make a physical connection. Loving touch reminds our kids that we love them unconditionally and that we are here for them. Being busy — living hectic lives — is all the more reason to make sure nurturing touch is always available. We need to make an effort to keep in touch, not only with our children, but with our spouses, partners, or any loved one in our life as well.

Parents of teenagers might be surprised to learn that adolescence is a time when a child's needs are very similar to those of an infant. As standoffish and obstinate as our adolescents may appear at times, they are in fact in need of even a little extra affectionate touch to remind them they are safe and cared for. Adolescents, struggling with the confusion of becoming adults, often find themselves fearing sex while at the same time craving the touch that might not have been available to them in infancy or throughout their childhood. More often than we might care to think about, teens may turn to casual sex as a replacement for the nurturing touch they are needing.

One mom, after becoming aware of how physically distant she had become from her adolescent daughter, began a new morning ritual. Instead of letting the alarm clock wake her daughter as usual, she began to take her morning coffee into her daughter's bedroom before the alarm would go off and sit on the edge of the bed. Slowly and gently she would stroke her daughter's hand until she awakened her from sleep. Both mother and daughter benefitted greatly from this physical closeness, paving the way for them to reconnect emotionally as well. There are unlimited possibilities for us creatively to bring healthy touch back into our relationships with our children. All we need to do is find them.

As essential as it is to increase our awareness of how we are parenting, it is equally important to understand that if our focus is always on our children our own life goes unnoticed. If we are focused only on ourselves, intimacy will elude us. One of the main objectives of this book is to remind us to maintain a healthy balance between the two. With that in mind, bring your awareness now to your own life. We've talked about sound, smell, sight, and touch. How are your senses being *touched*?

Could your ears use a little vacation? Consider turning off the loud music, the constant drone of the television or radio, and listen to the wind in the trees, the birds singing, soothing music, or your own inner silence. Treat your nose to something beautiful to heighten your awareness of the sweetness of life — like fresh air, fresh flowers, or fragrant incense. Turn your eyes inward and gaze upon the beauty of the inner landscape, or sit quietly watching the sun set while the last rays of light give way to the night.

Nurturing ourselves and others is like adding fertilizer to a garden: the flowers are more fragrant; the fruit is sweeter. How might you incorporate more nurturing touch into your life? Ask your partner for more affectionate touch or ask your friends for more hugs. Give more hugs yourself. Take a soothing warm bath and take time for foot rubs or back massages. Offer more foot rubs or massages to others. Physical activities like swimming, walking, or hatha yoga are also ways to be loving toward your body and to increase your awareness of its beauty, harmony, and grace.

The baby in us, that part of us that can get totally lost in the luxurious feeling of being touched in safe and soothing ways, is still there. We need to recognize and acknowledge that part of ourselves. When we do, we will find ourselves reconnecting to our natural and spontaneous inner Self from which all love flows.

Chapter Five

The less able we are to accept our own feelings and express them in healthy ways without attaching guilt or blame, the more likely it is that we will discourage our children from expressing theirs.

Most of us have been conditioned to look for quick answers to problems in our lives. What we hope to convey through this book is that lasting change happens gradually. It is a process that needs to be lovingly supported and nurtured, requiring continual reinforcement and steady reminders. We didn't get to be how we are in a day and we're not likely to change overnight. Still, it is only our understanding that needs to change. How long does that take?

Did you find it easy or difficult to bring touch into your relationships since reading the last chapter? Many people find that there is desire for nurturing touch, but there is also a block — a wall of fear, or resistance, or discomfort. One way to begin dissolving the block is to slow down, breathe deeply, and reconnect with the inner love. Ultimately, it is the power of love that dissolves the block. It is the power of love that makes it easier to give and receive touch.

Typically, instead of remembering that we are filled with love, we often confuse ourselves with our feelings, particularly the ones we label as negative. When we feel angry, we think that we are the anger. When we feel sad, we think that we are sadness. When we feel hurt, we think that we are the hurt. The more we identify with each of these feelings, the less able we are to experience our true Self — which is love. The more we identify with our emotions, the more we think we have to stop, deny, fix, or get rid of them. This is what leads to those insurmountable walls being built — the very walls that keep us from connecting to our inner love and to others.

Once, during a newspaper interview, a journalist asked, "How do we end up with so many negative feelings about ourselves anyway?" If our natural inner state is love, how and when did things go haywire? Later the same week, while sitting in the park, I witnessed a scene — all too familiar to me when my children were younger — that serves as a perfect illustration.

A mother, apparently angry and frustrated, was directing her pent-up emotions at her young children. As the scene progressed, she became increasingly hostile and aggressive, barking orders at her two sons, who appeared to be no more than four and eight years old. Frightened by her anger, the boys started scrambling to do what their mother was yelling at them to do; but no matter how hard they tried, they were unable to hold back the storm. As the tirade continued, their eyes began to reflect their mounting fear; their inner beings seemed to retreat somewhere deep inside; they no longer looked or sounded like children.

Finally, the woman lost control of her anger and started hitting her sons, all the while yelling at them for being disobedient. Her youngest boy began to cry, begging her to stop. Her response was to get angrier and demand that he stop crying — that he "shut up." The more she yelled, the more he cried. The more he cried and wouldn't — couldn't — stop his tears, the angrier she became that he wasn't listening to her.

The father, who had said nothing until this point, finally chose to speak up. He told his sons that they were responsible for their mother's anger, that they never listen that they never do what they are told. If they would just do what they are were told and mind their mother, this wouldn't happen. Further, they both had no business crying or complaining since this was all their fault, and they had better shut up, now!

How do we end up with so many negative feelings about ourselves anyway? How do we go from feeling so totally connected and enthralled with the world as infants to living in fear? When and how do we come to distrust our own feelings? Why do we stop living life spontaneously in the moment when it started out being so natural? Finding the answers to these questions may require taking a look at how we were raised. It also necessitates understanding what happens developmentally to all of us around the age of two.

Most of our parents had every intention of being good parents. Many of them assumed that simply providing food and shelter for their offspring was being a good parent. After all, taking care of basic necessities often required great effort and personal sacrifice. In their generation, not much was known about the psychological and emotional make-up of children.

What does being a good parent suggest? Does it mean having well-behaved kids who always mind and are always pleasant and cooperative? This is a commonly held assumption by many of us. If our parents believed this, and we have, over the years, held this up as the benchmark of successful parenting, it's quite likely we'll be in for a rough ride when our children turn age two, or again when they reach adolescence.

Can you remember what it feels like to be two years old, to move from the blissful state of "oneness" we all experience in infancy to the not-so-blissful state of being a two-year-old? When you finish reading this paragraph, put the book down; close your eyes and take a deep breath. Let yourself relax as you watch the gentle rhythm of your breath. With each exhalation watch the years melt away as you allow yourself to become younger and younger. Keep going back in time until you find yourself entering into the world of a two-year-old. If you are unable to reconnect with yourself at that age, do your best to *imagine* what it might have been like for you.

By the age of two we are more capable of doing things for ourselves — not to mention all the other things we *want* to do for ourselves. Much to our delight we walk, we talk, we feed ourselves, and we even try dressing ourselves. We are very curious about the world that we can now explore. We realize that we can express our needs; only they're not as simple as they once were. Our language, with its limited vocabulary, hasn't quite caught up with our thinking and feeling capacity, so we are often frustrated communicators. We also are beginning to recognize that there are "others" out there and that we don't always get the response we want from them.

It's a very stressful time for both us and our parents. As infants we viewed everything and everyone as extensions of ourselves. By age two we are starting to become aware that this is not how the game is played. We begin to recognize that we are separate from others, but we are also able to influence and interact with them. We are aware that our various responses get an assortment of reactions: one way of being might get us hugs and kisses, while another elicits a harsh word or a pat on the butt. Being spontaneous has become a risky business. By expressing ourselves, we risk not only disapproval and withdrawal of love but, in our own little minds, our source of food, shelter, and protection as well.

It is an emotionally taxing game for all the players. Our parents need to set limits on our two-year-old antics, enough so we can grow out of egocentricity and learn to be socially adept, yet not so much as to severely inhibit free expression. We, on the other hand, need to gauge our responses accurately enough to get our needs met and establish separateness without it resulting in rejection and abandonment. It's a game laced with anxiety and ambivalence, yet filled with adventure. It's the same game we'll play later on as adolescents.

As two-year-olds, we begin to test whether we really are different from the people we are noticing out there by being completely oppositional. When someone says yes, we say no. If they say go, we stay. If they say rest, we want to play. It's a surefire way to prove we are separate and that we have a mind of our own. Actually, we have no choice; it's built right into the system. Given what our developmental task is at this age — to establish that we have a separate identity — being obstinate is right on track.

It's truly quite amazing how intuitive and bright we are for being so young. As we're nailing down our confidence about being separate, we are also trying to figure out how far our influence extends with the grown-ups. Naturally, the smartest technique is to demand the most and work back from there. The game is: demand a lot and demand often. The response we get helps us understand and define our limits.

Next on the agenda is to figure out how our feelings affect others and vice versa. The answer to this question will also help us get a grip on how separate we are. So we observe: When I cry, do they cry? When I shout, do they shout? When I hit, do they hit? Or, when they cry, do they tell me I caused it? When they're angry, do they say it's because I made them that way? Yikes! No wonder we need naps and teenagers sleep in until noon: this is emotional calisthenics.

If the answer to these questions is usually yes, it's going to be very confusing figuring out where we stop and someone else starts, or to be able to recognize and separate our emotional state from everyone else's. On top of it, we'll more probably develop a healthy dose of guilt or shame for having feelings — anger, sadness, fear, sexual desire — if we see that it continually throws people into a tizzy.

Parents who are not firmly established in their true Self or not aware of their natural inner state of love — or who simply don't understand two-year-olds — will probably be taken to the limits of their endurance more than they care to experience. More than likely, they will react to their frustrated, demanding, angry, or sad children by attempting either to control them or overindulge them, while inadvertently experiencing their children's spontaneous emotions as compelling evidence that they are "bad" parents.

One important concept to understand is that our children's emotional states can, and often do, reveal our own unresolved emotions. If these old feelings were painful or remind us either consciously or unconsciously of a time we would rather not remember, our response to our children might be to discourage the healthy expression of their emotions, or even to be angry at them for having feelings. Mistakenly, we might think that we are doing a good job of parenting when really all we are doing is protecting ourselves from seeing emotions that bring up discomfort in us. The less able we are to accept our own feelings and express them in healthy ways without attaching guilt or blame, the more likely it is that we will discourage our children from expressing theirs.

Take a moment and reflect on what we have been suggesting so far and notice how you are feeling. Remember, when you are noticing you are not being critical, judgmental, or evaluating yourself — you are simply witnessing. Do you want to argue with us and tell us we haven't lived with your child or we'd know why you act the way you do? Do you feel subtle pangs of guilt or shame over how you've been treating your children? Are there feelings of anger or remorse? Do you find yourself dismissing the whole premise of this chapter? Whatever you are aware of is telling you something about yourself, so listen with your heart.

Be grateful that you have the opportunity to view your life from a new perspective. As you look with new-found compassion and respect at your children, find a way to acknowledge what wonderful and amazing people they truly are.

We'll develop this theme in more detail in Chapter Six. In the meantime, be sure to read this chapter often.

Chapter Six

When we are clear about our children's need to be emotional without it throwing our inner state off balance, we will spontaneously support the natural process of development.

In Chapter Five we were talking about the developmental changes that happen at age two and noted what a stressful time it is for both children and parents. There is no doubt that at this stage of life, parents who are not firmly established in their true Self, or not aware of their natural inner state of love — or who simply don't understand two-year-olds — will probably be taken to the limits of their endurance more than they care to experience. More than likely, they will react to their frustrated, demanding, angry, or sad children by attempting either to control them or to overindulge them, while inadvertently experiencing their children's spontaneous emotions as compelling evidence that they are "bad" parents.

Without realizing it, parents who are afraid of their children's budding assertiveness — or expression of feelings — will sometimes try to stop the process by scolding or hitting their kids. When this happens, the message conveyed to the children is that they are being "bad" or "naughty" for what amounts to being two years old. If this is done often enough, these kids may throw in the towel when it comes to expressing themselves and start assuming that they should feel and be what their parents want them to feel and be.

At this age, since children are still dependent on adults for survival, the pressure to conform is very intense. Even so, there are some whose temperaments are such that they refuse to throw in the towel. They demand a little louder and a little longer, desperate to prove their individuality. Power struggles that ensue from this type of parent-child conflict can get pretty ugly.

Not all of us attempt to stop our children's assertion of will by scolding or hitting. Some of us are inclined to view our children's sadness, anger, or demanding ways as evidence that we are doing a rotten job and that our kids don't really love us. Doesn't this sound familiar — unless our children are always happy, outgoing, and loving we think there is something wrong with us and that the way *they* feel is somehow our fault? Unfortunately, it's a heavy burden on our little ones when we subtly, or not so subtly, make them responsible for *our* feeling good.

What inner connection must we be missing that has us convinced our children have to behave a certain way in order for us to feel good about ourselves? What inner connection must we be missing that has us thinking or feeling we need our children's love, approval, and affirmation before believing we are doing a good job of parenting?

What may be missing is the heart connection — the connection to our inner essence, our inner love. It's when we're disconnected from our inner love that we find ourselves giving in to our demanding children — or trying to fix everything so that they never have to feel sad or angry and we can feel good about ourselves and our parenting. But watch out: it's all an illusion. When we indulge our children confusion will reign supreme.

Our kids have expressed their feelings or opposition to prove that they are different — separate from us — and we turn into a chameleon and become agreeable with them again. Spooky! Where does this leave them except to wonder if maybe they're not so separate after all, or that they must possess some magic power that makes the whole world adjust itself to them? If this happens often enough, children will grow up confused and ruled by their exaggerated emotions.

When children are controlled, manipulated, continually criticized, or overindulged, they learn to stop listening to their inner voice. They become disconnected from their inner essence and put their focus on what others feel or expect from them. All of the negative thoughts, feelings, and belief systems that they're exposed to get embedded in their budding definition of themselves: I'm bad or naughty; my feelings are wrong; I cause others to feel sad and angry; I'm not safe; I have more power than the people who are supposed to take care of me.

As children learn to shut off access to their spontaneous feelings like anger and sadness, they begin putting into place the mechanisms to ignore, deny, or repress their feelings. Before they know it, they've lost their ability to express themselves freely. They also begin at a very young age to cut off access to their natural inner state of love and bliss. The foundation of the wall we talked about in Chapter Four — that keeps us distant from others — was laid in many cases by age two. In families where children were abused or neglected as infants, the foundation was already laid in the first year of life.

In adolescence, children get a chance to play the whole scene over again. Some will dye their hair three shades of purple and wear fourteen earrings to prove that they are different from their parents. Others will continue to suppress their individuality and emotions and be in for an explosion of adolescent behavior somewhere in their thirties or forties. Worse yet, some will develop addictions to alcohol, drugs, food, shopping, exercising, working, etc., as a means of self-expression. Regardless of the form it takes, the inability to express pent-up feelings of anger and sadness can leave kids feeling chronically depressed and block their access to inner love and joy.

So this is one answer to the questions posed in Chapter Five: How do we end up with so many negative feelings about ourselves? If our natural state is love, how and when did things go haywire? It happens when we are shamed for having what amounts to natural and spontaneous feelings. Once our feelings are accepted as okay, as simply part of life, we can learn not only to express them without hurting ourselves or others, but to see them as a source of deeper understanding about our individuality and our needs.

In the next several chapters we will propose over a dozen positive approaches to discipline that will make it possible for children to have their feelings, yet maintain appropriate boundaries on them. Consistently using these approaches will help our kids begin to master their emotions instead of being controlled by them. It is something we need to consider as well.

In the last chapter we asked you to try reexperiencing what it was like to be two years old. If you couldn't get into that exercise, how about this: What happens when *you* have oppositional, angry, sad, fearful, or sexual feelings? Do you repress or deny them, or shame yourself for having them? Do you indulge yourself and feel you have the right to get whatever you demand and have everything fixed immediately? What happens when others express their feelings of anger and sadness? Do you take the blame or lose your inner sense of tranquility? Do you sometimes feel like your very survival depends upon pleasing everyone around you and always being good? Are you constantly in power struggles, still trying to prove your right to be an individual by never cooperating or compromising? Being two years old might be more familiar than you originally thought.

If we are operating out of the space of an emotional two-year-old when we discipline our children, what do you suppose we are role modeling? Consider the woman in the park described in the last chapter. Haven't we all been there? When our "two-year-oldness" starts to rise up, our fears have gotten the best of us. Instead of giving in to the fears we need to keep our attention focused on *our* reaction to our children's behavior — not the behavior itself. We need to feel whatever we're feeling in that moment without judgment or blame and courageously let the emotion pass through us. It may be we need to leave the room to safely express ourselves or to lovingly offer ourselves consolation. Whatever we do, we need to keep our feelings separate from our children's while we find the inner balance to discipline with emotional maturity.

This is what self-discipline is all about: taking responsibility for our feelings and doing what we need to do to get them into balance. When we practice self-discipline we are remembering that we are not our feelings, but the witness of our feelings. We may feel angry, but we are not the anger; underneath everything — whatever we are thinking or feeling in the moment — we are still love. Remembering the truth will also begin to dissolve whatever we are afraid of. Once the fear is dissolved, we will be able to let our children express their opposition, frustration, anger, or sadness without shaming and judging it. There will be no reason to read their feelings as statements about us: that we are bad parents or that we are unloved or unappreciated.

By the same token, when we have oppositional feelings or anger or sadness we can learn to express those feelings. We can and must learn to freely express ourselves without blaming anyone for how we feel and without hurting anyone or anything by our expression. Setting the example is what will teach our children — even if in the beginning we fail more often than we succeed. Simply saying, "I'm sorry, I didn't have the right to yell or hit you; I was angry and I'm still learning how to express my anger; I may make mistakes sometimes," will go a long way with our children.

Breathe through the guilt or shame that comes up and let it dissolve. Many of us are still two years old at heart and not very good at expressing our feelings. We need to be as patient with ourselves as we are with our children.

As you read this chapter, try to keep in mind that all feelings are acceptable though we may have been taught the contrary. Even anger is okay. Not surprisingly, anger indicates that we have deep feelings about something. It lets us know that something inside has been violated, that we are afraid or that a need is going unmet.

The same is true with sadness, although anger and sadness

are two emotions often confused. In our culture, men will typically express sadness as anger, and women anger as sadness. This happens because we have been conditioned to believe it is more acceptable for men to be angry than it is for them to be sad, and women to be sad than it is for them to be angry. In any case, we only *feel* sad; we are *not* the sadness. Sadness is usually about a loss that cannot be fixed. It is a feeling that must be recognized and accepted for what it is. We can feel the sadness, recognize our loss, and ideally integrate the experience into a greater awareness of how everything constantly changes except our inner love.

When we are clear about our children's need to be emotional without it throwing our inner state off balance, we will spontaneously support the natural process of emotional development. We will no longer feel the urge to fix, control, or indulge our children because of our own feelings. We will be free to be separate individuals connected through our inner state of love. What a wonderful example to set for our children.

Please review Chapter One.

Chapter Seven

If we are able to change our assumptions about why our kids misbehave, we may be able to choose more positive discipline strategies.

In the upcoming chapters we will explore the topic of discipline. Have you been remembering to make self-discipline a part of your everyday life? Disciplining our children clearly makes more sense if we are living a disciplined life. We're not making this up — it's really true! Still, there are some important things to know if we want to save both our kids and ourselves a lot of grief.

We have already seen some of the ways we get our buttons pushed and how this causes us to react or overreact out of frustration to our children's emotions and behaviors. Ideally, becoming aware (conscious) of the dynamics involved has made some difference in our approach with our children. If we take a moment to think about it further, we may also notice that we often punish — yell, threaten, or hit — our kids when we disapprove of their behavior or have been pushed to the limits of human endurance.

Who isn't guilty of disapproving of their children's behavior at one time or another — maybe even frequently? The fact of the matter is, much of our disapproval is the result of having unrealistic or inappropriate expectations for our kids. We are more likely to get annoyed or frustrated with our children when we *think* they're doing what they *shouldn't* be doing or not doing what we think they *should* be doing.

Gradually, we will make our way through the various stages

of childhood. If we *know what to expect,* or at least have a better understanding of what "normal" behavior is for each stage
of development, life will seem much less demanding. So much
tension and unhappiness comes from not having enough information to work with. If we look back at our own families, how
many of us grew up adequately prepared for what we are experiencing now? There are many of us who aren't quite sure what
normal (healthy) behavior looks like.

Learning socially appropriate behavior is probably the most
difficult thing a young child will ever have to accomplish.
Understanding social norms, expectations, and etiquette — or
how to live in the world without getting everybody upset —
not to mention the task of controlling appetites, impulses, and
aggression, takes insight, intelligence, and self-control. It takes
years to refine these traits, and some of us are still working on
it. Are we not?

Consider how often we whine at our kids to stop whining,
or the many times we snap, "Just a minute, I'm busy, be patient!" because we're too impatient to set our own task aside
for a moment to respond to our children. How often do we nag
about developing good eating habits and not watching trash on
TV, only to find ourselves slouched in front of the tube stuffing
ourselves with junk food the minute our kids are in bed?

These examples are not an indictment of our behavior —
only a reminder to give ourselves a break now and then. So,
don't our children, who are much younger and less mature, deserve the same? Yet for some of us this behavior is more than
occasional; it's the way we typically operate. When this is the
case, disciplining our children will look more like "Do what I
say, not what I do," and may be the biggest reason why it often
doesn't work.

Learning socially appropriate behavior is harder than learning to play baseball, ride a bike, or play the piano. When our
kids drop a ball, fall off their bikes, or hit a wrong key on the
piano, do we threaten them, hit them, or yell at them and send
them to their room? Ideally, no. Instead, we comfort them and
encourage them to try again. When possible we show them

how they might be able to do better the next time, or simply let them know that we all make mistakes. Wouldn't it be wonderful if we could maintain this attitude when they make mistakes in their social and emotional behavior as well?

It is not uncommon to find, as we discussed in Chapters Five and Six, that our assumptions about our kids' behavior are not always accurate. If we believe that our children misbehave only because they are naughty or because we aren't good enough parents, our thinking is too negative and we're going to end up feeling miserable. This is when we are more inclined to use "power" tactics like yelling or hitting to get the quickest results.

Not only does this set a poor example for our kids, but most of the time we end up feeling guilty. It drives a wedge in our relationships with them and does nothing to teach acceptable, age-appropriate social behavior. On the contrary, it leaves our children confused and disheartened without the inner resources necessary to become self-disciplined.

If we are able to change our assumptions about why our kids misbehave, we may be able to choose more positive discipline strategies. This one shift alone will help raise our children's self-esteem, foster more loving relationships, and teach them to respond to difficult situations in healthier ways.

The following is a partial list of underlying reasons for "misbehavior." We suggest rewriting the list, preferably in a bold colored magic marker, and posting it where it will be readily visible at those times when your patience is exhausted. In time, you will undoubtedly connect with your own intuitive sense of what to expect from your children.

Why Kids Misbehave*

1. *They are immature!* This isn't meant negatively; our children simply haven't lived as long as we have. Consequently,

---

*List headings are from Clare Cherry, *Parents, Please Don't Sit on Your Children* (Belmont, Calif.: David S. Lake Publishers, 1985).

they have neither the cognitive nor emotional capacity to do some of the things we think they should be doing. For instance, a two-year-old doesn't know how to share; a three-year-old isn't capable of picking up and putting away all his toys; a four-year-old doesn't know the difference between a lie and the truth in certain situations; a fifteen-year-old doesn't have the foresight to consider the ramifications of all her behavior. A good rule of thumb to remember is, whenever you feel tempted to sputter, "You should know better!" to your children, stop and ask yourself just *how* and *why* they should know better. Perhaps they have never been taught patiently enough or often enough to do what is expected of them. Or maybe they just aren't mature enough to master the task yet without help.

2. *They are bored!* Some boredom for children is healthy and leads to creativity and relying on their own resources. It isn't our job in life to keep our children entertained twenty-four hours a day. However, many kids are bored because their natural sense of imagination has been dulled by too much television, too many toys, and too many hours in shopping malls. We get into ruts with our children because our imagination and energy level have been stunted. Boredom in our kids may be a call for interaction. Many of us need to reawaken our own imagination, wonder, and playfulness. We hope that reading *The Essence of Parenting* will become a constant reminder to slow down and get more in the game with our kids.

3. *They are curious!* Kids get into all sorts of trouble checking things out. We're not suggesting that we let our kids get into anything and everything their hearts desire; but recognize curiosity as curiosity. Punishing it will only squelch their natural desire to learn things for themselves. When we find our children investigating where they don't belong or without regard for the consequences, we need to provide them with the necessary guidelines. Setting boundaries consistently and with love will bring about the greatest results.

4, 5, 6. *They are hungry, tired, or coming down with something!* So much unnecessary stress could be avoided if we

kept attuned to these three culprits: hunger, fatigue, and illness. Many mothers have called 4:00 p.m. the arsenic hour.
Providing healthy snacks between meals is a simple solution.
Moreover, it's probably healthier both physically and emotionally to eat small amounts frequently in response to feelings of
hunger than to eat three big meals a day in response to the
clock. A quiet time amid a busy day to sing, tell a story, or
give a back rub can prevent a lot of crabby behavior. And who
among us has not scolded our children mercilessly for their
whining only to find out a few hours later that the crankiness
was due to the onset of a fever or the flu? None of us is above
making this mistake. If we can remember to consider the pos-
sibility of illness before beginning to scold, we will reduce the
odds of reacting in a way we may regret later.

7. *There is a family crisis!* Kids are emotional barometers
who naturally measure the pressure in the house and act it out
for us. They are like sponges soaking up everything that's going on around them. Children are uncomfortable with stress
and try to get rid of it any way they can. If we see a lot of un-
explainable "bad" behavior, we may need to take a good hard
look at what's going on with the grown-ups. Is there tension in
the marriage? Work-related or financial stress? If we are personally dealing with depression, anxiety, or an addiction —
alcohol, drugs, food, work, spending, sex — our children will
know it and feel it.

One of the most tragic things we can do as a parent is to ignore our inner state and how we live our life as a contributing
factor to our children's misbehavior. Many children are busy
acting out our frustration, anxiety, or unhappiness — and then
getting punished for it. In other words, our kids end up paying for what we are unable to manage in our own lives. They
become our whipping posts. All of our focus and attention become centered on their behavior rather than the source of the
problem, which lies within us. This particular reason for our
children's misbehavior is the most difficult to look at. Recognizing it means admitting that we need to work on difficult
issues in our life. Even if this brings up great fear and resis-

tance, facing *our* problems is crucial if we hope to transform our life and bring lasting harmony and joy to our families.

This concludes the first part of the list. Use it frequently by referring to it whenever you think your children are misbehaving. If it seems like one of the seven reasons listed fits the situation, see if you can come up with a creative solution of your own; or try one of ours. For example, in response to boredom: take a trip to the library; have a fifteen-minute conversation; start a new hobby together. In response to curiosity: consider posting rules or supervising a simple investigation of the *fascinating* subject. Observe your family's eating and sleeping patterns to see if there is a rhythm to the day that will prevent overtiredness and hunger.

Another way to use the list is to notice how these same influences are affecting you. Remember, this book is about us as much as it is our children. We need to become aware of *our* level of emotional maturity and whether our expectations for ourselves are reasonable. For example, do we give ourselves room to make mistakes as we learn the art of being human? Is boredom prevalent in our lives? Is it time to explore a new interest, talent, or social experience? Do we need to give more attention to our primary adult relationships and maybe bring them back to life? Do our own sleeping and eating patterns negatively affect our outlook and responses to our children? Are we living healthy, balanced lives?

So get the list up and have fun with it. There's more to come.

Chapter Eight

Parenting is more than having good skills. It is more than just being devoted to our children and wanting what is best for them. It cannot be separated from any other part of our life. Whatever is affecting us, regardless of how obvious or subtle, is also affecting our children. Whatever exists in our life also exists in theirs.

We are not assuming that everyone reading this book wants to be like or live like the "Brady Bunch." *The Essence of Parenting* is not about creating an "Ozzie and Harriet" family. We are aware that most people reading this book do not live in fairy tale or Hollywood families. More often, they live stressful lives, sometimes under heartbreaking conditions, with frustration, hopelessness, and unhappiness their constant companions. Fortunately, all that may be necessary to stimulate change is new information, a different perspective, and the knowledge that we are not alone.

Throughout the years of teaching and counseling we have come to know hundreds of individuals and families intimately. We have laughed and cried together, sharing in the suffering and tragedy as well as the joys and triumphs. We have felt the pain, sadness, anger, fear, and loneliness as people have poured out their hearts. We have seen the scars of their unhappiness etched in their faces and lodged in their bodies.

The people we are referring to are ordinary people. They may live next door to you, or they may live in your house. They may even be you. To the rest of the world it appears as if everything in their life is "fine." They raise their families, go to work, do the shopping, clean the house, and maybe even go to a house of worship every week. No one ever suspects that they live their lives in fear: afraid of intimacy, afraid of losing control, fearful and mistrusting of relationships. Confusion and depression may often leave them feeling overwhelmed with life, estranged from the world, or even suicidal.

Most of my life I considered myself very lucky to have come from a happy, typical middle-class family. My brother and sister seemed to have emotional problems; but I always thought I was fairly well adjusted. I felt badly for my brother and sister and wondered how it was that they were so affected by our family while I had grown up so nicely.

One day I was sitting with a client reviewing a list of common characteristics usually associated with coming from a "dysfunctional" family. I had been over this list dozens of times with people, very astutely and compassionately pointing out to them the various ways they had been affected by their families. Usually I felt very fortunate, if not a little smug, about being so well adjusted. This day, however, the farther down the list I went, the more I realized the list was describing me. For the first time in my life I had to admit that I shared the same problems and traits as everyone I was trying to help.

As many times as I had talked with people about the problems in their families, I honestly never thought it applied to me. With this dropping of denial came a recognition of many areas of my life that were out of balance and in need of attention. Some of them were obvious and easy to admit to, like my explosive temper or the depression that would frequently throw me into fits of despair and gloom. Others were more subtle and not so easy to admit to, like fear of authority figures or being overly self-centered and selfish. What mattered most was that these characteristics and feelings had been influencing and affecting me my entire life. They had always been there, but I had been unwilling to accept them as part of me.

Once the initial shock passed, I wanted to point the finger at my parents and blame them for everything about me I considered to be a problem. It took some time before I could understand that the "problem" did not lie with my parents or anyone else; the problem was in me. Once I was able to admit that something *in me* needed to change, change became possible. With the dawning of this understanding, I was finally free to begin learning how to love and accept those parts of myself that so persistently stole my happiness and contentment. Becoming aware was an important step in changing my life.

I remember one middle-aged man who was trying very hard to make sense out of his childhood experiences in order to improve his relationships with his children and learn why his marriage had failed. He told me that his father had been a highly respected teacher in a parochial school who, many people thought, lived an exemplary life. In addition to the normal duties of a teacher, his father had also volunteered countless hours to numerous community projects. What people didn't know about the man was that almost every evening when he returned home he would beat his wife and children.

The person who shared this painful secret with me had never told another living soul about his father. His marriage had failed when his children were still young and he had been unable to develop a close relationship with them; he had been prone to violence and moodiness, unable to trust or to share himself emotionally. Fortunately, he eventually met a woman who insisted that he seek help before she would agree to marry him. With her support he was determined to break the cycle of his family history and free himself from the tyranny of his past.

Many people we know have experienced rape, incest, or other forms of physical, mental, and emotional abuse while growing up. Others have lived with the absence of love and nurturing through parent neglect or abandonment. For some of us the abuse or neglect continues in our lives as an ongoing reality. When this is the case, learning new parenting skills or techniques alone is not enough to overcome the impact these conditions have had and continue to have on our emotional state and our relationships.

Parenting is more that having good skills. It is more than just being devoted to our children and wanting what is best for them. It cannot be separated from any other part of our life. Whatever is affecting us, regardless of how obvious or subtle, is also affecting our children. Whatever exists in our life also exists in theirs.

The essence of parenting includes the willingness to look at ourselves to find the source of whatever we think isn't working. It may appear as if circumstances or problems are caused by our children or our partners, but in reality, they originate within us. This is not an easy concept to understand, but it is true. Blaming our parents, spouses, or anyone else is barking up the wrong tree. Only when *we* take responsibility for our lives, especially how we think — knowing that the power to change lies within us and in what we choose to believe — will our everyday reality improve.

The important thing to remember is that change is possible. Contentment and harmony are not mythical concepts: they are attainable by everyone. The essential factor is our willingness to make an effort to face ourselves and our life, head-on. We cannot ignore thoughts that leave us feeling inadequate, incompetent, or unloved, feelings that need to be expressed or relationships that need to change. To do so only perpetuates the very things we are trying to overcome.

We must also realize that these thoughts and feelings are what determine our reality. The more we focus on them and the more we believe that they describe us, the more a victim of their influence we become. Thoughts, feelings, and consequently conditions in our life are perpetuated only by strongly believing in their validity. They are true only if *we think* they are true.

If we believe we are incompetent, then we will have numerous opportunities in our life to experience that we are incompetent. If we believe we are unlovable, then we will probably see that reinforced with almost everyone we meet: no one will seem to like us or want to be our friend, including our children or our spouses. If we think we're stupid, or that we can't do anything right, or that we always make mistakes, it will seem like people go out of their way to point that out to us.

Rather than focus on everything we think is wrong with us, our children, our spouses, or the world, we can begin to focus on what is right about us. Instead of blaming others or our past, we can take responsibility for what exists in our life. The great spiritual teachers, not to mention modern-day quantum physicists, tell us that our thoughts are what determine our reality: change the way we think and we change our reality. This knowledge is something that we must begin to incorporate into our lives, to remember every day as often as we can. We are good people. We try hard. It is possible for us to live happy, contented lives feeling satisfied and fulfilled.

How much longer can we ignore our inner state? How much longer can we live our lives accepting and allowing negative thoughts and feelings to sour our disposition and steal our happiness when it is within our power to change them? How much longer will we condone, by our inaction, painful or stressful circumstances and conditions that drain our energy and enthusiasm for life?

The essence of parenting includes taking care of ourselves. It is not a selfish act to put our inner house in order. The more we attend to our needs, recognize and accept whatever feelings we are having, and remember to love ourselves just as we are, the more joyful our life, let alone our parenting, will become. Our children, after all, learn more by following our example than by listening to what we tell them. As we take care of ourselves, we take better care of our children. When we take care of ourselves we give them the message that they are *worth* taking care of.

In the upcoming weeks, remember to take time to slow down. Sit quietly, even if only for as long as it takes you to read this chapter, and breathe deeply. Allow yourself to let go of all your tension and worry. Feel the love that lies beneath all your habitual thoughts and feelings and remind yourself that you really are okay.

Chapter Nine

It takes courage, humility, and love to begin to open our hearts and live in the world without insisting that our way is the best or only way.

Let's continue with the list we started in Chapter Seven. Wasn't it a lot like being reminded of what you already know? The eighth reason provides an interesting perspective and is often a great source of relief and validation for parents.

Why Kids Misbehave (continued)

8. *Children have their own temperament!* Coming to understand and appreciate our children's (not to mention our own) temperaments can be an enlightening endeavor. Since ancient times and in all cultures, people have recognized that there are different personality types. To live in harmony with one another we need to acknowledge and respect each other's natural tendencies.

Native Americans, East Indians, Sufi saints, and Western psychologists and philosophers all have their own unique and beautiful interpretations of the personality types. Each one is profound and more far-reaching than we could possibly lay out here. To explain in depth the concept behind temperaments would require several volumes.

For our purposes, we have chosen a European perspective from the German philosopher Rudolf Steiner. According to Steiner, there are four basic temperaments. Each temperament, as illustrated below, can be understood by observing the characteristics of a season of the year, color, and element of nature that correspond to that temperament. To understand the "mood" or "flavor" of each temperament, picture the qualities of the corresponding season, color, and element that typify the nature of that personality.

Each temperament, if nurtured in heathy ways, gives rise to unique strengths and talents. However, the opposite is also true. If negatively reinforced, each temperament can become a burden. Although we experience some of each, all of us have a primary temperament. The same is true for each phase in our life: childhood/sanguine, adolescence/choleric, midlife/ melancholic, and old age/phlegmatic.

choleric
summer
red
fire

sanguine		melancholic
spring		autumn
yellow		violet
air		earth

phlegmatic
winter
blue
water

Like the season of summer when all of nature is at its peak time of blossoming, the *cholerics* are almost always bursting with life and energy. With bright and intense temperaments, cholerics are usually hot-tempered and aggressive in their actions. Often the life-blood of their family, classroom, or office, they keep things alive and moving — much like the circulatory system in our bodies. Children of this temperament need positive outlets for their energy along with ample opportunities to be physically active. Lovingly supported, choleric children can become great leaders and adventurers willing to meet any challenge head on with creativity and enthusiasm. On the other hand, if misunderstood — labeled as "bad" because they won't sit still — continually restrained, or disciplined with harshness (adding fuel to the fire), choleric children can become destructive.

Opposite the choleric temperament is the *phlegmatic*. Associated with the season of winter, phlegmatics have a dreamy, sleepy quality about them. Similar to the color blue, they are calm and placid. The nature of phlegmatics embodies the qualities of water. Outwardly calm, moving slowly and steadily, there is an unseen depth: "still waters run deep." Like the glands in the body that work at a deep level, there is more to phlegmatics than meets the eye. True and loyal friends, they have a profound respect for tradition and are often seen as pillars of society. While cholerics are busy "throwing out the baby with the bath water" to effect change, the phlegmatics will move ahead cautiously reminding us to hold on to what is good and true. Many times misread as dull-witted or labeled non-assertive, they are keen observers who typically would rather watch the game than play themselves. Phlegmatics need to gently be encouraged into activity or they risk becoming lazy, which could hurt them socially or physically. It is *not* their nature to do anything quickly — so patience is essential.

The *sanguine* temperament is reflected in the mood of spring: lively and changeable. The bright, sunny qualities of the color yellow also characterize the warmth and lightness of this nature. Like air, the sanguine personality is light and carefree, moving from one social situation to another with grace and ease. The sanguines' happy nature is an asset that makes it easy for them to get along with people and to put others at ease. Their bodies may also appear light, with a wispy, fragile, or even frail quality to them; even their overall health may be fragile. The nervous system of the sanguine temperament is alert, aware, and sensitive to its surroundings. Because of their keen ability to pick up on many things at one time, sanguines are often socially adept. The flip side is they can also appear to be flighty or scatter-brained. Too much activity can accentuate their nervousness. Sanguines often require encouragement to remain focused as they have a tendency to jump from one activity to the next, leaving things undone.

Opposite the sanguine temperament is the *melancholic*. There is a heavy, introspective quality about these individuals, who by nature appear to carry the weight of the world upon their shoulders. Often perceived as being pessimistic and dispirited, melancholics feel things very deeply and are touched by the suffering of others. They enjoy being *in their feelings* and can seem morose and sad, loving nothing more than a good cry. As with the season of autumn, there is an underlying sense of the coming darkness and death. Like the earth itself and the color violet, the alluring, dark nature of melancholics has a deep, rich, and beautiful quality. Possessing great strength and depth, this temperament is most associated with the body's bone structure. Filled with sensitivity and compassion, melancholics are more than willing to listen to a sad story, making them potentially great caregivers. If caught in their own introspective woefulness, however, they may become overly self-pitying. Their feeling nature is both a marvelous asset and an Achilles' heel.

As the body needs all its systems to operate fully, as nature needs each element to maintain balance, as every season has its own purpose, and as color brings beauty and richness to the world, so too does humanity need people of each temperament. Each one of us has our own unique but limited perspective on life, and it is essential that we live our life true to our own nature. Trying to be someone we are not is not only unfulfilling; it creates feelings of incongruity and unhappiness that can lead to depression and addiction. We must overcome the powerful tendency to fear or to want to change or fix what is different from us. It is possible to accept and learn from our differences instead of always trying to change them. As the Native Americans so aptly put it, we need to walk in each other's moccasins.

Can you imagine a choleric mother trying to get a phlegmatic child off to school in the morning, or a phlegmatic mother cooped up all day with a choleric child? Without understanding or appreciating each other for who and what we are, the inclination might be to punish our child or force him to change. How can a child change his nature? Forcing him will only lead to shame and frustration for everyone involved.

The phlegmatic parent needs to understand the choleric child's exuberance and find healthy and acceptable outlets for her energy. Similarly, the choleric mother may need to understand that the phlegmatic child will probably need more time than she herself takes to get ready in the morning, possibly requiring gentle encouragement and numerous reminders to keep him moving from one task to the next.

Understanding our own temperament can be life transforming. Many of us are in need of balancing our temperament as well as letting go of being overly identified with our own limited perspective. It takes courage, humility, and love to begin to open our hearts and live in the world without insisting that our way is the *best* or *only* way. We need to look beyond the outer differences and find the love we all share, to learn how to live from love's perspective.

9. *Children are sensitive to the food they eat and other things in their environment!* We can hardly pick up a paper or turn on the news without hearing about a new study on the effects of pollutants and additives on our health, mood, and behavior. A lot of aggressive, irritable, and inappropriate behavior can be linked to our children's diet and environmental allergies. We are not suggesting that we immediately run our kids to an allergist (although in some cases medical treatment might be necessary) or that we live in a plastic bubble. We simply need to be aware that too much sugar, chocolate, wheat, milk, or mold may be contributing to our children's crabbiness on a given day. Screaming at or spanking our little ones won't help. Too much external stimuli — like what kids experience in malls, in front of TVs, or with video games — can contribute to irritability. Try balancing these activities with quiet time or playing outdoors to discharge the build-up of excess stimulation.

10. *Too many "nos" and "not nows!"* Kids need opportunities to experience both patience and disappointment; but it's probably worth our while to become aware of how many times we unnecessarily respond in the negative. Almost any no can be phrased as a yes. "Can I have a cookie, mom?" "Sure, as soon as we've had dinner," instead of "No, not now!"

Clearly, children need limits and to hear no at times; but we may be overdoing it. How many times do we say no to a child's fun idea simply because we've lost *our* spontaneity or have *our* priorities mixed-up? Too many nos and not nows frustrate children and can lead to rebellion or withdrawal.

Try two yeses for every no. "No TV tonight, but how about a game of monopoly or taking a bike ride together?" "I'm sorry there isn't enough time for a picnic today, how about we plan one for next week or stop for ice cream while we're running errands this afternoon?" Be creative and lighten up.

11. *We reinforce their negative behavior!* We probably do more to encourage misbehavior than discourage it — especially if we've been parenting unconsciously. Think of how many times we pay little or no attention to what our kids are doing until they act out. What a time to give them our attention; we've just rewarded misbehavior.

12. *Misbehavior is "masked" behavior!* Surely we've all heard the story about the man who kicks his dog because he's mad at his boss. It's a good illustration to keep in mind when we see our children misbehave. Often kids hide hurt, sad, or scared feelings behind a punch, shove, or smart-aleck comeback. It doesn't mean we tolerate the misbehavior, but only that we need to become more attuned to our children's unspoken feelings. Addressing the feelings makes more sense than punishing children.

13. *Children need to test limits!* Kids *need* to test our boundaries, or limits, to find out how far they can go. If our boundaries are healthy — not too rigid and not too weak — we'll be able to respond calmly and lovingly to the testing. If not, *watch out!* Either our kids will be walking all over us, having no respect for themselves or us, or they'll have no sense of themselves — and the unlimited possibilities that await them — because they're squelched every time they act spontaneously.

Children who have no sense of themselves (identity) may begin looking for one by experimenting with sex, alcohol, or drugs as they get older. If we feel threatened and resort to screaming and hitting when kids test us, or if we feel used and give in when our kids test, it's time *we* develop healthy boundaries. We should be thanking our children for making us aware of how wishy-washy or unclear our boundaries are, not punishing them.

We hope you are not overwhelmed by the list. It is not intended to be a diagnostic tool so we can identify the *real* reason our children are misbehaving and then administer the *correct* solution. The list is only a resource to inspire us as we go about the business of shifting our perspective and opening our awareness. It is intended as a useful illustration of the wide variety of reasons children sometimes act the way they do.

Whatever the reason for our children's behavior, it's probably nothing to be afraid of or feel threatened by. Most importantly, the reason usually doesn't warrant punishment; it warrants discipline. The question is, is it our child who needs the discipline, or do we?

So the next time the kids act up, slow down and breathe deeply. Let the list dance in your mind. Let it erase the thoughts about your child being bad, or about you being a bad parent. Approach the situation with thoughts about the innate beauty and goodness within both you and your children and watch what spontaneously unfolds.

Don't forget to add this list to the other one and post it.

Chapter Ten

Our job as parents is to find and stay connected to our inner essence so that we can always see and respond to the beautiful inner essence of our children.

In the last chapter we completed a baker's dozen list of possible reasons for misbehavior. Now seems like a good time to lay out what we believe are the three primary goals of discipline: to teach the desired behavior, to maintain our child's self-esteem, and to preserve a respectful parent-child relationship.

As we become more conscious in our parenting, our disciplining techniques ideally will nurture the development of self-respect, healthy interpersonal relationships, and problem-solving skills. Gone will be the knee-jerk reactions to our kids' behavior, the increased blood pressure and the modeling of our own erratic behavior. To accomplish this, however, will require several things on our part: self-discipline, practice, patience, and a sense of humor.

Most of us have been living our lives believing that our inner state — thoughts and feelings — is determined or controlled by circumstances and forces outside of ourselves. If someone does something we deem negative or unacceptable, we get upset. If someone says something hurtful or critical, we feel terrible. But there is no outside force shaping our emotions or our reactions to situations; it is all happening inside of us. Once we recognize this and really know it, all it takes to shift from an undesirable state of mind to a positive one is a subtle shift in *will*. In the same way, a subtle determination to change our responses will, in time, produce the desired results.

Changing our behavior will not be easy if we try to force the change. We need to be as patient with ourselves as we hope to become with our children. At first we might catch ourselves after we've reacted in the same old way and regret a missed opportunity. Then we might catch ourselves right in the middle of an old response and not be able to make the shift quickly enough. Eventually we'll *see* the old pattern rearing its head in time to try something different.

New responses might feel foreign in the beginning, but sooner or later they will become as natural as yelling and punishing have been. Well, almost. It is, however, unreasonable to assume that children who were trained to expect scolding and threats will respond immediately to new techniques. It may take some time, but anything worthwhile does. Believe in what you are doing and keep trying.

The first positive, down-to-earth discipline technique we recommend requires a tremendous amount of trust: trust in the innate goodness of our children, trust in letting go of control, trust that our inner state and exemplary role modeling will have a profound effect on our children, and trust that everything will turn out all right.

Keep quiet and say nothing. It's shocking to realize how much of what we say to our kids is negative and critical — a reflection, perhaps, of our attitude toward ourselves and the undisciplined state of ruin our minds have fallen into. Children who are continually criticized feel badly about themselves; and children who feel badly about themselves, misbehave more often. Most of us would see a change for the better in our children's behavior if we would simply remain silent.

Some of us will protest, "But if my child does something wrong, I should point it out to her so she doesn't do it again!" Granted, explaining appropriate behavior in a loving way is a positive discipline technique, but nagging and criticizing are not. Silence is actually preferable to nagging, scolding, or criticizing.

Isn't it true — the more you monitor someone's behavior, the more mistakes that person makes? Think about it. Did you ever take a typing class in high school? My fingers would fly across the keyboard until Sister Mary Margaret Matilda stood behind me and watched. Suddenly, I was all thumbs. The same is true for our kids. They become self-conscious, ill-at-ease, and lose their self-confidence when constantly watched or bombarded with negative messages. They also stop listening to their own inner voice and start paying more attention to external sources.

Keeping quiet requires great trust. When we see our kids doing something wrong or inappropriate, it's normal for most of us to think we have to comment. After all, if we don't intervene and correct the situation, our kids are going to turn out horrible. Right? Not so. The alternative is to trust in the innate goodness of our offspring, trust that our example will serve as a stronger guiding force than being critical or judgmental.

Whenever I would take my kids to a playground and they would begin climbing on the slide or the monkey bars, I'd start squirming because of *my* fear of heights. I'd hover and shout warnings, telling them what I thought they should be doing. All this did was make them more self-conscious and nervous. Instead of listening to their own internal warning system and sense of balance, they started listening to me and my fears; they lost their confidence. Instead of listening to their own bodies, they doubted themselves.

Children at ease with their own bodies will know how far to challenge themselves and will even fall and recover gracefully. My job as a parent was to make sure that they were playing on safe equipment, that they knew some basic safety rules, and that I was available if they needed me — not to shout instructions. I gradually learned to let go of my own fears and joyfully watch them play. The same principle also applies to children's social behavior.

How much negative or critical talk is there on any given day? Buy a bag of rubber bands slightly smaller than the size of your wrist and carry them around in your pocket. Every time you say something negative or critical to your children (or partner), slip one on your wrist. By the end of the day you will have a tangible example of what all your negative talk has done to your children's self-image and your relationship to them; it's choked the life out of it. If your arm begins to turn blue, stop the experiment; you've proven the point.

So are you with us? Let's say you've conceded the point and are ready to remain still at that critical moment. Now what? In those moments of restraint we suggest you try witnessing your thoughts. That's right, just watch them; don't get involved with them. Entering into the state of "witness consciousness" is the easiest way to replace redundant negative thinking with a still mind. With practice you will find it both relaxing and rejuvenating. It will also lead to a more positive state of mind from which to discipline.

Did you know that at least 90 percent of what we think every day we've already thought before? Very little of our thinking is original. What's even more amazing is that most of our thinking comes from unnecessary worry and the replay of negative or critical messages from our past: our parents, Sister Mary Margaret Matilda, Grandma Bessie, Aunt Sylvia, and even Coach Boor.

Another great way to keep silent is to stay focused on the truth: at our essence we are love. Nothing is going wrong; everything is okay. Some of us will still argue, "The truth is my kid is misbehaving!" That may be a fact or current reality, but is it the truth? For something to be the truth, it must be absolute. It must be true not only today, but it should have been true one hundred years ago and must still be true one hundred years from now. One hundred years from now will it be true that our children are misbehaving? Will it be true that at our essence we are love?

This may be a hard concept to grasp because some of us think we haven't experienced our inner love yet. The truth is, however, it's always been there, but somewhere along the way we got disconnected. Our job as parents is to find and stay connected to our inner essence so that we can always see and respond to the beautiful inner essence of our children. This isn't always easy when our children are misbehaving. It's even more difficult if our children don't fit the world's criteria of "beautiful" because of some physical or mental disability they were born with or developed later in life.

Once you start to get a handle on biting your tongue and reducing the negative commentary, we have a few more practical suggestions to try with your little ones.

Offer gentle reminders. Before going into new or difficult social situations, offer positive pointers instead of nagging or scolding after you get there. "Remember at Grandma's house we keep our feet on the floor and use our inside voices. Say, 'Yes, please,' or 'No, thank you' if she offers you a treat. I know you'll do a great job; you're polite kids." Your children will see you as an ally rather than a drill sergeant.

Use gerunds. Gerunds are the "ing" form of a verb. The gerund of "walk" is "walking." Use a gerund to tell your children what you'd like them to do rather than nag about what you want them not to do. The human mind is not equipped to make pictures of the negative of something. So if you say to your children, "Don't walk in the street," their minds will make a picture of walking in the street and their behavior will likely follow suit. However, if you say, "Walking on the sidewalk is safer," a picture of the same will be generated and you'll be more likely to see the desired behavior. "Playing nicely is more fun"; "Closing the door quietly is a good idea" — it really works.

Try nonverbal reminders. If our children develop nasty habits that need adjusting, we can find nonverbal ways to bring them to their attention. For instance, your daughter may be in the habit of whining. Each time she whines you can try combining the gerund "talking nicely" with a gentle stroke on the cheek. After a time you can eliminate your comment completely and let the gentle stroke on her cheek serve as a reminder to change

her tone of voice. Nonverbal reminders can confidentially remind our kids to curb a bad habit without drawing attention or
comments from brothers and sisters who are in earshot.

Self-discipline, practice, patience, and a sense of humor —
remember? These are just a few of the tools we need as we
go about the business of becoming conscious. It has been said:
Becoming conscious requires both self-effort and grace. With
even the slightest adjustment in our attitude, grace rushes in.
So try the rubber band trick; watch your thoughts; practice silence and replace nagging with one of the suggestions offered
so far. See if you can strengthen your connection to your inner
essence by spending time with it daily. Remember to reward
yourself for your efforts.

Chapter Eleven

We need never stand in judgment of ourselves or others. Our parenting is uniquely our own and cannot be reproduced by anyone; nor can we reproduce anyone else's.

Two books I've enjoyed reading to my children are *Little Women* and *Little Men*. I am so touched by the love that inspires the parents in these books — love nurtured like a tiny ember that is the only source of heat for survival in the midst of a raging blizzard and is dangerously close to going out; love both tender and firm, self-sacrificing, yet infinitely fun and mischievous, even outlandish at times by ordinary standards.

The feelings these books inspire in me are akin to the opening of the heart: floods of adoration and tenderness toward my children; appreciation for the beauty of childhood as a time of innocence, joy, and awe; gratitude for the privilege of participating in the unfolding of these young lives; delight in their discoveries, the excitement of life seen through their eyes; a sense of being blessed as the recipient of their love and trust. What could be more rewarding in life? Yet how often I take my relationship with my children for granted, or treat it casually, instead of recognizing it as the ember: so precarious, so fragile, so easily diminished if not given my constant attention, protection, and encouragement.

It is difficult to continue recommending the specific discipline techniques that logically would appear in this chapter. The list is coming and will probably prove useful to almost anyone who begins to incorporate it into their child-rearing practices. Yet a part of me loathes the list. I hate how it can be

misinterpreted and misused. I hate what it can come to sym-
bolize. I want to scream: *"Techniques are not it — Our state of
mind is!"*

My resistance toward even offering the list comes from not
wanting in any way to insinuate that there is a "right" way
to parent. A list can become a trap; it can become a burden;
it can be just one more criterion we measure ourselves against
and fall short in comparison to. Or we can go through the mo-
tions rigidly and self-righteously complying with it, smugly
thinking we are better than those who don't. Lists can lead to
judgments, and judgments only take us further from our inner
essence.

There was a time in my life when I used lists a lot, thinking
I was going to be the ideal parent. It was a grand and noble
delusion; and all my lists only perpetuated the delusion. There
is no one right way to parent; each of us must find our own
right way. Out of a foundation of love creative, intuitive, and
unique responses to our children will spontaneously arise. A
list of techniques is only as valuable as the love that inspires its
implementation. If love is already abundant, the list becomes
secondary.

In my heart I longed to create a beautiful life for my children.
I dreamed of being infinitely kind, patient, wise, generous, and
full of fun and spontaneity. I wanted to fashion myself after
the mothers I read about as a child in novels like *Little House
on the Prairie, Little Women,* or *Little Men.* I wanted to be like
Julie Andrews in *The Sound of Music.* I had my longings, my
dreams, my good intentions. My "list" faithfully reminded me
of goals to achieve, yet I found myself failing miserably at my
attempts to incorporate these techniques or virtues into my life
naturally.

It was a struggle to be consistently positive and good na-
tured. I often felt false in my attempts, strained. I felt frustrated, guilty, and inadequate when I failed, despairing when
my actions were noticeably inconsistent with my intentions.
In my frustration and anger I would wonder: How is it I am
not the kind of parent I want to be when I have the best of

intentions? I am well informed; I have my lists; I love my children.

By an act of grace, I came across a book called *Self-Esteem a Family Affair* by Jean Illsley-Clarke (Minneapolis: Winston Press, 1978). The author proposes five affirmations that all children need to hear in order to be established in self-love and acceptance; so, I immediately added the five affirmations to my "lists."

Over time, as I worked with this new list in my own life and as I talked to other parents, a light suddenly went on inside of me. I might have been able to verbalize the affirmations to my children, to pay lip service to them out of sentimentalism, or when I was is a good mood, but not until I was living the affirmations would they truly be transmitted and take root within my children's hearts and souls. I realized that I could not give to my children what was missing from my own life.

With the dawning of this new understanding, I turned the affirmations around and began applying them to myself. I decided that it was time for me to become established in self-love and acceptance so that I had something real — rather than a cheap copy of someone else — to offer my children. Eventually, working with the affirmations led me to a threshold where, with a leap of faith, I was able to shift my parenting out of the realm of *doing* and into the realm of *being*. Through determination, self-effort, and grace I finally came to understand: I don't do mothering; I am mothering. I need never stand in judgment of myself or others. My parenting is uniquely my own and cannot be reproduced by anyone; nor can I reproduce anyone else's.

We want to share the affirmations with you now, not as another list of to-dos, but as a gift. We hope you can accept this gift with love and compassion: the spirit in which it is being offered.

1. *You have every right to be here!* We all do. Each of us has a right to be here, even if we don't always feel that way. Stop and ask yourself if you honestly believe that you are cherished for no other reason than the mere fact you are alive. Whether you feel that way or not, it is still true; and it is wonderful that you are here. Yet how many of us have come to measure our worth by what we produce, how much we accomplish, how much we earn, how much we do for others? When did we start believing that just being wasn't enough?

Many of us have spent our lives trying to prove we are worthy of respect, that we have earned the right to just *be*. Subtle or not so subtle messages from our childhood may still be playing in our subconscious, telling us that we are unwanted or that our feelings, ideas, and experiences are invalid, unimportant, or not good enough. We may feel like a failure, or hate ourselves because we don't measure up to someone else's standards — or perhaps our own. It is crucial that we uncover and uproot all of these messages and become firmly established in the deeper truth that at our essence we are all the same. From love's perspective everything is okay. We are good people; we try hard; we deserve to be happy.

2. *You don't have to hurry!* In order to experience that deeper part of ourselves we must make the necessary effort — which leads right up to a second affirmation: We need to slow down and spend time with that part of ourselves that is beyond the doing, the thinking, the feeling — that part of us that just *is:* the "silent witness." So much of the time we are rushing around, racing here and there, trying to juggle, trying to catch up. It's not only our bodies that are in constant motion; it's our minds also: busy forming opinions and judgments about ourselves and others; busy planning, plotting, worrying, and doubting. When we maintain this frantic pace mentally and physically, we end up consuming life rather than savoring it. Our lives take on the quality of junk food rather than the flavor and ambiance of a carefully prepared feast to be relished and enjoyed at leisure.

Slowing down may seem scary to some people, impossible to others. We might not accomplish everything on our lists, but it does afford us the opportunity to recognize and experience the truth: that we are acceptable and lovable because of our innate value as human beings, because of what exists within each and every one of us. We don't have to be *human doings* to justify our existence.

Slowing down and spending time with ourselves will lead to a greater awareness not only of the feelings that lie just below the surface, but of those we have tried to keep buried as well. The most common reason why so many of us never take the time to slow down is that subconsciously we are trying to keep all of our uncomfortable and painful feelings under wrap. Often we are numb and don't realize it. We think we know who we are when actually we haven't the faintest idea. We can't tell you how many people over the years have admitted to us, "I don't know who I am; I don't know what my feelings are."

When I first tried slowing down it was painful to be with all of the agitation, judgments, worries, and ruminations that constantly ran through my mind. My instinct was to run from everything I was experiencing, yet somewhere deep inside I knew the time was approaching to face myself. Sooner or later, I had to face the task of sorting through and untangling the jumbled state my mind was in so that I could let myself feel what I had been unaware of or avoiding for so much of my life.

Without realizing it, my freedom and spontaneity had been lost in a sea of negative thoughts and emotions. Now, to free myself from their influence, I had to learn to sit patiently and witness all that had been blocking the doorway to my heart. If I wasn't willing to look, how could I possibly ever know that "I" was different from all of the beliefs and feelings that ruled my life.

Once we have stopped identifying ourselves with all the unnecessary thoughts and feelings that have stolen our happiness and contentment, we will achieve an openness that allows rushes of love to spill forth into our everyday life, spontaneously and effortlessly. To become established in this inner love we must consciously spend time with it.

Sit or lie in a comfortable, relaxed position. Turn on some gentle, soothing music. Wrap yourself up in your favorite blanket or climb into your favorite rocking chair. Breathe deeply and slowly, allowing the tensions of the day to drain away. As thoughts come up, watch them dissolve as though written in chalk on the sidewalk and washed away by a gentle spring rain.

Take however long you need to let yourself become still. Take as much time as you need to find the warm inner radiance that lies beneath all your surface thoughts and feelings. Bask in it, revel in it, and know that we all share this inner space. Even if you are unable to reach the inner radiance this time, keep trying. It is your very own treasure waiting to be discovered.

What did you notice when you closed your eyes and turned your attention inward? Was it hard to keep your eyes closed? Did your mind shift into turbo? Did feelings start to surface: anger, worry, agitation, sadness? If they did, you're off to a good start. They were simply feelings there for you to notice.

Through the process of slowing down, it becomes evident that in our daily rushing around many of us have neglected some basic needs. Maybe we were simply too busy to take time for ourselves. Maybe we never realized we had needs — especially if they were ignored or denied in childhood — or perhaps our busyness has been a subconscious tactic to keep us from realizing our needs because we are afraid or ashamed to admit we have them.

3. *Your needs are okay with me!* If we expect and hope that our children will learn to listen to their needs, that is, their inner voices and their bodies, and report them honestly so that they can be adequately met, we cannot role model while ignoring or denying our own needs. If we act like saints by pretending not to have needs, what are we telling our children about their acceptability as human beings with needs? Our only real choice is to demonstrate that having needs is not something to be ashamed of; it is simply a part of being human. We must also role model a willingness to tell others what we need as part of demonstrating how to take care of *ourselves* in loving ways.

If we are willing to take the time to slow down and listen, we'll begin to notice exactly how and where we lost touch with our personal needs. You think you don't have any? How about the need for adequate rest, nutritious food, exercise, play, spirituality, healthy relationships, dreams, and intellectual growth? Or how about the need to let ourselves experience the full richness of our humanity: love, joy, fear, anger, sadness, loneliness, and sexuality?

In those precious moments of quiet, when our attention is drawn inward, we *need* to listen to the sweet refrain of our own heart's song.

Chapter Twelve

You have every right to be here. You don't have to hurry. Your needs are okay with me. I'm glad you're a boy; I'm glad you're a girl. I like to hold you. These affirmations are more than words; they are gifts we must offer ourselves time and time again to feed our hearts and souls. They are a gateway to our inner love: the foundation of all we do as parents.

We ended Chapter Eleven talking about the need to let ourselves experience the richness of our humanity, including our sexuality. To understand and appreciate the dynamics of our sexuality is an essential part of living and parenting consciously. Embracing our sexuality — which comes after we have healed and matured emotionally — allows us to participate in the eros aspect of love: the creative, rejuvenating, expressive energy that nurtures our spontaneous self.

Sexuality: the joy of embracing and appreciating our sexual selves. How many of us can say we admire and enjoy our bodies and our sexuality? Most people we know have thought about trading their bodies in for a new model at one time or another. How we are sexually says more about our emotional health than almost any other aspect of our lives.

4. *I'm glad you're a girl* or *I'm glad you're a boy*. This was perhaps the most difficult affirmation for me to face. I may not have been living the other affirmations, but at least I could change them behaviorally. The confusion and frustration I felt

about my sexuality and my sex life — about being a woman —
was rooted in shame. Basically I felt totally inadequate. I had
learned to shut down my sexual feelings long ago as a child.

To hide my shame I convinced myself that sex wasn't that
important in a relationship. My husband and I had mutual love
and respect; and occasionally we had sex. The experience was
usually frustrating for me: my body didn't respond, or if it did,
I felt guilty. I told myself that I much preferred affection to
having sex.

It was also during this time in my life that I struggled with
depression and extreme irritation and anger. I was constantly
judging other people's behavior, feeling like I was being short-
changed in most of my relationships. Until I had to face the
affirmation "I'm glad you're a girl," I never knew there was a
correlation between by emotional state and my sex life. What
was true for every other aspect of parenting had to be true for
sexuality as well: children learn what they live. If they live with
shame, they feel shame. How could I hope to raise three children to feel good about their sexuality when I didn't feel good
about mine?

My personal journey of exploring and embracing my sexuality brought me face to face with every emotional issue that was
undermining my happiness. What I came to realize is that our
sex life is a symbol of our entire emotional life. Our sex life is
one predictable arena where all the symptoms of our wounded
and immature emotional state get played out.

Many of us have been raised to not talk about sex. Yet,
here we are talking about it. Take a minute to notice how you
are feeling right now. Are you relieved? Anxious? Interested?
Are you feeling open to the topic, or guarded? Remember just
to notice. Becoming conscious is a matter of awareness, not
judgment.

Since sex is typically such a taboo subject in our culture, many
of us don't know how to gauge whether what we are experi-

encing in our sex life is healthy. In case *you* were wondering, here are three simple criteria to get you started.

First, both partners are having sex as often as they'd like to. When I first started teaching and doing therapy, it seemed that most women complained that their husbands wanted sex more often than they did; they were too tired and too busy with the children to answer their husbands' sexual demands. Obviously there are times when we are genuinely too tired to have sex. However, if we've been too tired for months, or even years, isn't it time we took a closer look at what's really going on?

Maybe we're not fatigued at all, but depressed. On the other hand, if we truly are physically and emotionally wiped out, what does that say about how well we are taking care of our personal needs? In either case, sex doesn't have to add to our exhaustion; it can be a remedy to soothe fatigue, release tension and stress, and rejuvenate the body. Is it really fatigue, or is fatigue just a cover for the deeper issues contributing to our lack of physical and emotional intimacy?

In recent years, we have noticed that more women are now bemoaning that their husbands neglect them sexually — their husbands are working too hard at their jobs, are too engrossed in the TV, or have simply shut down emotionally and sexually in the marriage. Men feel a lot of the same things women do: fatigued, inadequate as a sexual partner, confused about their sexuality, pressured in their role as a provider, and often under great societal pressure to perform or get left behind. In addition, our culture has not been kind to men in supporting them emotionally or encouraging them to be vulnerable — both critical ingredients for a healthy emotional and sex life.

Realistically, both partners are not always going to be "in the mood" for sex at the same time; one or the other may have a stronger sex drive and desire sexual interaction more frequently. However, many of us typically sit in silence, unable or unwilling to reveal the build-up of feelings: hurt, disappointment, anger, resentment, frustration, rejection, loneliness. Others harshly express their disappointment through criticism. Both people in a relationship need to be sharing with each other what they are feeling and needing.

It is vital that each of us recognize the impact this breakdown is having on our relationship with our partner and begin to take steps to share how we're feeling. Not being touched affectionately, not sleeping together sexually for months or years at a time, not being able to enjoy or embrace our physical, sexual self may leave us feeling empty and disheartened instead of content and fulfilled. Needless to say, there will be a spillover into other areas and relationships in our life.

The second criterion is that both partners are able to express their needs. In general, women have a more difficult time knowing what their sexual needs are. Little girls are given stronger messages about not touching themselves than boys; and their genitalia are more difficult to explore. Our culture is more likely to accept that a boy will play with his penis while bathing or urinating. No such allowances exist for girls.

Women are also given stronger messages that it is unnatural, or at least unladylike, to consider and act on their own sexual needs and desires. If women act sexual or want sex, they must be cheap or immoral. Women have been taught that their role sexually is to respond to and please men, but only if they are married. After twenty or thirty years of these messages, it's difficult for us to suddenly become free and spontaneous in a relationship.

Developmentally, our erotic nature begins to emerge in adolescence. Ideally, this would be the time to begin identifying and responding to that nature. Unfortunately, there is no safe, acceptable way in our culture for men or women to explore their sensuality and sexuality. In some cultures, young men and women may go off alone and perform rituals of dancing, body painting, or some other self-expression to discover their own unique sexual energy. In our culture, watching R-rated movies, looking at pornography, or becoming sexually active are often the most common outlets teenagers have for exploring their sexuality. Tragically, these outlets are typically exploitive, confusing, and can be emotionally damaging.

As a result, many of us find ourselves entering into relationships not really knowing or appreciating our bodies or our needs. Yet, regardless of what each of us brings to the relationship from our upbringing or cultural conditioning, it is important that enough honesty and vulnerability exist to safely explore the uncharted territories of our sexuality while we learn to express our needs openly without blaming or demanding anything from our partner.

The third measure is that our sex lives are dynamic: constantly growing and changing. Our sexuality is an expression of *ourselves* and the love we experience in our relationships. If we are growing and changing personally, then our relationships will too; and all of this growth will be reflected in our sex life. Conversely, a flat, ritualistic, predictable sex life may indicate, among other things, emotional rigidity and excessive control.

The point of all this is not to make sure everyone is simply having a great time in bed. Our sex life, as we said earlier, is symbolic of our emotional life. A healthy sex life requires the same ingredients as a healthy emotional life: trust, vulnerability, honesty, the ability to know and express our needs, spontaneity, letting go of control, and the willingness to take charge of our life and our body. If these ingredients are not evident in our emotional life, they cannot be manifest in our sexual life. In the same way, if they are not manifesting themselves in our sexual life, it is because we have not nurtured them in our emotional life.

Sex can become dry, empty, and boring. It can also be a source of personal pain or used as a weapon to manipulate others. We can fool ourselves into thinking there is a right or wrong way to be sexual and either judge ourselves, or others, for not measuring up. We may hide our fears, sexual addictions, affairs, or impotence because we think it's our fault things are not working. Think again. In the end, sex — like the *list* — is only as meaningful as the love that inspires it. It is the love we must access! This does not mean running around making love to everyone, but that in finding this love, we can feel drunk with joy and intense delight wherever we are or whomever we're with.

The love we are talking about is not a sappy, sentimental love or love that comes and goes like a good or bad mood; it is not a love that we portion out in different measure to different people. It is that profound, eternal, expansive energy that vibrates in the silence and penetrates all life; it is the field of energy out of which everything flows. It is our very own Self, our essence. We can feel intoxicated and fully alive, open to all the excitement and beauty of life, yet able to hold it within us like a secret smile.

So what does all this have to do with parenting? Only that our greatest task as parents is to use every means at our disposal to find and stay connected to our inner love.

How often are we too busy, too preoccupied, to gaze into our children's eyes, to reach out and pull them onto our lap, shower them with kisses, press our cheek against theirs and lose ourselves in the rapture of love? The love is there; it's usually that we're too tired, burned out, depleted, or hurried to be aware of it. To recognize our inner love, we must spend time with it!

5. *I like to hold you!* As we become more comfortable with our sexual self, we naturally tend to become more comfortable and generous with our affectionate self. Remember in Chapter Four when we talked about the importance of loving touch. Here it is again. There is no substitute for human touch. Whether it's hugs or gentle caresses, massages or pats on the back, touch affirms our connection to each other. It releases stress; it soothes the soul; it makes us glow. When we are hugged we breathe deeper; we become more aware of what we are feeling; we are drawn more fully into the present moment.

We can't demand hugs from others, but we can ask for them. We can also treat ourselves to nurturing touch by soaking in a warm bath, snuggling in a cozy blanket, rocking in a chair with soft music on, or lying in the grass basking in the sunshine. When we slow down and take care of our need for touch, it becomes easy and natural to offer it to our children.

You have every right to be here. You don't have to hurry. Your needs are okay with me. I'm glad you're a boy, I'm glad you're a girl. I like to hold you. These affirmations are more than words, they are gifts we must offer ourselves time and time again to feed our hearts and souls. They are a gateway to our inner love: the foundation of all we do as parents.

Chapter Thirteen

If we can hold in our minds that our children are basically good, doing their best, entitled to slip up now and again, and that their behavior is not a reflection on us, our approach to discipline will be transformed.

Self-discipline, practice, patience, and a sense of humor — remember? Not a day goes by when these don't matter. Actually, we're amazed at some of the thoughtless things that still escape our mouths after all these years. If we drop our vigilance for even a moment, they reappear like a pimple the night before a big date.

In Chapter Ten we laid out what we believe are three primary goals of discipline: to teach the desired behavior, to maintain our child's self-esteem, and to preserve a respectful parent-child relationship. With these goals in mind, we're now ready to continue with some practical suggestions on how we might change the bad habits *we* have developed into positive behaviors that will improve not only our children's feelings about themselves, but their behavior as well.

These are only suggestions. Try them out; they might work. At the very least, they are entertainment for the mind. Without the *heart opening*, they're just more things for us to think and worry about.

Anticipate trouble. If we take the time to notice, most of us will find that our children present the same problems over and over again. We're on the merry-go-round right along with our kids reacting to these problems again and again in exactly the same way. Very little changes. In some families, it's arguing about shoes left lying in the middle of the floor; in others it's kids fighting about where they get to sit in the car; or maybe it's fighting about whose turn it is to use the car Saturday night.

Once we begin to notice there's a pattern to the madness, a simple solution is to anticipate the trouble and *change the environment* in which it occurs to prevent it from reoccurring; many of us have simply not thought about it. We're more used to sitting back hoping things will magically go more smoothly the next time, only to get upset and yell or complain or punish our kids when the same old problem arises.

There are several easy ways we can change the environment in order to prevent difficult situations from reoccurring. First, *we can enrich it.* Take the case where children begin to fight out of boredom, say on a long car trip. A ready supply of pipe cleaners, books on tape, crayons, paper, and travel games will cover many miles. Be creative. Take along old photo albums no one has looked at in a while. Then, instead of three hours of listening to children fight and whine "Are we there yet?" you can reminisce about the past.

At times, the opposite works best: *impoverish the environment.* Transition times are difficult for kids, especially young children. Many parents assume they can horse around or watch TV until bedtime and still expect junior to hop right into bed and go to sleep. Children need time to unwind from being active or bombarded with stimuli. Turning off the TV, providing a warm bath, reading or singing to a child snuggled in bed before the lights go off all can help to eliminate bedtime hassles.

Simplifying the environment is particularly useful for the younger child who is mastering skills. If spilling milk is a common occurrence and drives you crazy, use the "tippy" cup. If getting your two-year-old dressed in time so you can get the five-year-old off to preschool is a power struggle, put him to bed in sweats so he's already dressed when he wakes up.

Child-proofing the environment is also a must for little ones.

Children under the age of three are not capable of self-discipline. We need to be their guardians, making sure that whatever is within their reach is safe and unbreakable. Homes where toddlers live should be an interior decorator's nightmare: nothing of value should be below waist high. A toddler's task in life is to investigate; our job is to make it safe for her to do so without getting scolded or having her hands slapped for touching things that can break (like everything electronic).

This doesn't mean our whole house has to be a disaster area. An important tactic in changing the environment is to *restrict certain areas.* If we need a place that's clean and orderly, we should make it off limits by putting up a gate for toddlers and enforcing the rule with older children. Sometimes we need to restrict the area for reasons of cleanliness, that is, if we don't want the carpet and furniture in the living room ruined, we can make it a rule that children cannot eat or play there. Don't let them take food there with the instructions not to spill it. You know that doesn't work, and you'll end up angry and scolding them. We have a right to make areas off limits for loud play, rough play, messy play. Just be sure that there is a place somewhere in the house where they are free to be kids. The key to effecting change is that we begin to notice where the commonly occurring patterns of troublesome behavior are and then come up with a creative solution that can be put into play before the trouble begins; if it works, we're geniuses. Most solutions typically fail, by the way, because we're inconsistent or give up too soon, not because our kids are hopeless or incorrigible.

Call attention to positive role models. This technique requires that we have more than one child or a very well behaved pet. It's the technique some of our really clever teachers used when we were in school, and it goes something like this: Almost everyone in the class is jumping around, chattering, paying absolutely no attention when the teacher calmly announces, "Mary, since you are sitting so nicely, you may be the first to go out to recess." Suddenly everyone is sitting nicely and hoping to be the next one called. When one child is acting out, compliment a child who is behaving. Most kids will improve their behavior in order to receive praise.

Be careful with this technique. It's not a good idea to compare children: "Mary, look at how nice Billy is sitting; why don't you sit that way?" Also, it's not wise to keep using this technique if it becomes evident that you're always using the same child as the positive model. This can inadvertently accentuate sibling rivalry and undermine the self-esteem of both children. Be sure to offer praise to the child who makes the shift in his behavior, immediately afterward, even if the move toward more positive behavior is only minor.

Use humor. We all get into ruts of being crabby and irritable. Practice *lightening up.* Put a sign where you first look in the morning — on the bathroom mirror, your spouse's back — that says "Be Cheerful" or "Be Optimistic." A cheerful attitude can be successfully cultivated if we choose to work on it. Cheerfulness can transform our experience of any situation. When we are light and cheerful we are living in the space of the heart; when we are dark and gloomy we are caught in the seductive drama of our life, taking everything way too seriously.

Realistically, some of us may have trouble lightening up. Maybe we're of a melancholic nature. Maybe we're addicted to depression, worry, or fear. Maybe we believe if we don't control everything — our spouses, our children, the details of our life — nothing will turn out right. Maybe we don't even know why we take everything so seriously.

Whatever the reasons, it's worth changing our outlook. If it takes going to see a therapist, then we need to do that. If it means finally accepting that we came from an alcoholic family, or still live in one, or that we were abused or neglected as children, then so be it. Whatever is stealing our happiness and contentment, whatever stops us from living with spontaneity and humor, is not worth holding on to. Why put if off any longer? There are too many excellent therapists, support groups, self-help books, and caring people in this world to live another day trapped in a never-ending cycle of humorless monotony.

Offer choices. Have you ever caught yourself sounding like a drill sergeant? Sometimes when my children were younger, I would notice my tone of voice — the harsh impatience — and shudder. I would hear myself barking commands or making dictatorial demands on my kids: "Pick up!"; "Get dressed!"; "Let's go!" Compliance on their part was based mostly on fear and the undeniable message that they didn't have a choice in the matter. Besides being less harsh, less overbearing, and less frightening, I could have been gentler and more polite: "Please pick up."

More than that, we can build in choices for our children: "It's time to pick up. Would you like me to read you a book when you are through, or give you a big hug before you start, or put on some music while you're doing it?" The issue is no longer whether our kids will acquiesce to our demands, but rather how they will go about doing what is expected of them. When they have some choice, some control over the situation, they usually feel better about complying with our request.

Choices notwithstanding, children under the age of five learn best by example. If we want our child to learn to pick up his toys cheerfully, we need to be engaged in the task alongside of him. Setting an example is also important as our children grow older. If they never see us cheerfully doing the same tasks we're asking them to do, how can we expect that of them? A child who sees his father doing dishes is more likely to do dishes when asked.

Offering young children certain choices under specific circumstances is, however, quite different from allowing children or expecting children to make major decisions at too young an age. Many of us do our kids a disservice by allowing them to choose things when they're not ready mentally or emotionally to make such choices. They simply shouldn't be burdened with the job of sorting out and weighing consequences until they can see the bigger picture.

Many parents have been frustrated after letting their three-year-olds choose, for example, to take ballet lessons, with a big investment of time and money in the class, the shoes, the outfit — only to have the ballerina lose interest and no longer want to go to class. Exercising our parental prerogative is not always the easiest thing to do, especially when we don't want to be the bad guy. Several years ago, my younger daughter wanted to stop playing the clarinet after sixth grade because she disliked the band teacher. If the decision had been left up to her, she would have quit on the spot. Our position was that she try seventh grade band for one semester since we knew the middle school had a truly outstanding band program. Then if she still wanted to quit, we wouldn't stop her. Even though she was angry and fought us for days on end, she ended up loving band and continued to play for two full years.

Encourage. Instead of criticizing or coercing our children to do better — "Come on now, you should know better; it's easy to get this" — we need to empathize with them. Statements such as "I know this is difficult," or "I used to have trouble with this too" do more to strengthen their inner confidence and will achieve better results than telling them that something they're already struggling with is simple. It's obviously not simple for them or they wouldn't be struggling with it.

Clarify messages. Clarifying messages is a positive strategy that requires discipline on our part. Instead of moaning, "This house is a pig sty," try "The bathroom sink needs scrubbing, the garbage needs emptying, and please make your bed before you run out to play." Instead of yelling, "How many times do I have to tell you not to jump on the bed?" how about "Jumping on the bed is not allowed; come down now."

Basically, there are a few good rules of thumb to follow when instructing children to change their behavior or to do something for us. The first is, be sure to have their attention. Rather than hollering up a flight of stairs, we need to go where the child is and get on eye level. Next, be sure to use words they know and avoid sarcasm. The third rule of thumb is to give them a time frame. Lastly, consider their developmental capability: Is what we're asking a reasonable expectation? Check in with the child to be sure the message got across.

Offer positive rewards. Instead of punishing children for what they do wrong, encourage them to do what is expected by building in a positive reward. Some people think this is bribery, but don't we all want rewards for the work we do? A bribe is given to someone to coerce them into doing something unlawful. All we're suggesting is finding a tangible way to acknowledge and reinforce our children's efforts. Using a positive reward system gets us more focused on the positive efforts rather than the negative ones. The payoff does not necessarily have to involve money, food, or toys. It can be as simple as a trip to the park, playing a game of their choice, or a visit with a special friend.

This approach is very positive for everyone. Eventually, children feel good about learning the new behavior and no longer need external rewards. It becomes reward enough to complete the task, especially if that means more quality time with us. The next time you are about to threaten, "No story if you don't get into bed right now," try "Two stories if you can be in bed in less than a minute."

Ignore negative behavior. If our child is not doing anything to endanger another person or someone's property, we can try to ignore her behavior. The challenge with this technique is that *everyone* in the house must consistently ignore the behavior until it disappears. Unfortunately, as the child tries to provoke a response from us, the behavior will typically get worse before it gets better. If anyone gives in and pays attention to the behavior, we have to start the ignoring process all over again, and it will probably take longer to work the next time. If you think you can follow through, this is a good one to use on temper tantrums or whining.

Temper tantrums are developmentally predictable around age two and age seven. However, they can also be signs that our child is overstressed or that there is unexpressed anger or overcontrolling behavior in the household. It is always amazing to me how many parents battle their child for control of the house. If we get hooked in a struggle and find ourselves overreacting in word and action, what in *us* is reacting so strongly? This isn't to say we should forget about ignoring the behavior; it just means that in all fairness to our child measures should also be taken to eliminate the stress or resolve the tension. Our children are truly masters at showing us where *our* weaknesses are.

When a child is in the throes of a temper tantrum it may be helpful to follow these suggestions: do not say anything to the child; do not look at the child; do not display an emotional reaction; do not allow your body to become tense; try to remain calm; remember to breathe.

When the tantrum is over, hug your child and talk about how he or she is feeling right then: "Looks like you are feeling better now." Avoid referring to why and what the child did. Remember, temper tantrums are a child's way to regain control when they are feeling out of control with a situation or feeling. It is unlikely that they understand what or why they were doing what they were doing. Distract the child to a different, soothing behavior, and try to forget about it yourself! If the child is hurting himself, others, or property while having a tantrum, it may be necessary to hold him. Try to remain calm and reassuring: "You're angry now; I'll hold you until you feel more relaxed." You may have to put the child in a separate room to keep her safe and away from others. You know best what your child will respond to. The key is to remain calm and loving; your inner state will eventually affect your child.

Take a break. Sometimes, the best thing we can do to deal effectively with whatever is overwhelming us is to leave the situation. If our children are old enough to be left alone for a while, a short vacation to our own room to rest, a warm bath, reading, or listening to music can all do wonders for our attitude; later we can reenter the situation with a clear mind. In Chapter Two we indicated that meeting or not meeting everyone's needs (ours included) in healthy ways is what determines the emotional climate of the household. If we're honest with ourselves, we have to admit that a lot of crabbing at our kids occurs because we are worn out.

Call a timeout. Many parents have turned timeouts into punishments. They grab their child and forcibly throw the little guy into his room while shouting angrily, threatening a timeout. When used correctly, timeouts are not punishment. Sometimes when kids are acting unsociably they need a break to recenter themselves, to quiet or calm down, to rest. It is in this spirit that timeouts, or renewal times, should be offered. For example, "You're having a hard time getting along with your sisters; you need some time alone until you can feel happy again and rejoin the group."

We need to be careful not to banish children to their room every time there is conflict or sad or angry feelings. Children have a right to their feelings and need opportunities to express those feelings as well as work through conflict. Still, there are times when a child has had enough and needs time alone to regroup internally. If our child completes a timeout and is still unable to reenter the group cooperatively, we can add a little more time.

Incidentally, timeouts are not appropriate for children under the age of three. We might have to remove a child from a particular situation that is too overwhelming, but to expect children that age to learn to cooperate by taking a timeout is unrealistic. Developmentally, they are not yet fully social beings. Demanding that a young child sit alone quietly is also unrealistic and often results in unnecessary and unhealthy power struggles.

Enforce consequences. Enforcing logical consequences is an important way to teach our kids to be responsible and to demonstrate that there are limits and boundaries to all behavior. Before putting a consequence into place, however, it is helpful to give our children a warning, not a vague threat: "If you do that again, you're really going to get it!" If we are disciplined disciplinarians, a warning should be given once and only once; then we need to follow through. A warning should be clear and realistic. It is helpful to state the misbehavior, the rule that has been broken, and the consequences: "You're home at 6:30. The rule is to be home for dinner by 5:50. If you are late again, you will have to stay home after school for two days to help remind you of our family's schedule." We must follow through if our children are going to trust and respect our word.

When choosing a consequence, it must be reasonable and fit the offense in type and magnitude and not be based on the mood we're in. I remember one mom saying she told her son he had to quit all extracurricular sports for the year because he was fighting with his brother; and it was only September. Overkill breeds resentment. Kids will focus on the unfairness of the consequence, which in this case was punishment, rather than learn from the experience.

It is also best if we can hand out a consequence in the spirit of helping and caring. By enforcing a rule, we are helping our children to learn their boundaries and establish inner controls. So be calm and matter-of-fact. Avoid yelling, criticizing, insulting, and name calling. Make the conflict be between a sensible rule and the child's behavior, minimizing as much as possible any personal conflict between ourselves and our child. When we punish out of hostility, our children see vengeance rather than justice. If we are always screaming, our children will learn to only take us seriously only when we're enraged, so stay calm. Remember, whenever we set a boundary we should expect that it will be tested; that's just life with kids. We aren't doing it wrong, nor are our kids defective because they grumble. If possible, enforce a consequence privately. Having siblings or friends in on the discussion can lead to teasing, humiliation, and efforts to save face. This is between our child and us. We can show our children respect by talking about the problem where others cannot hear and put in their two cents worth. Our kids may not say so, but they will appreciate our discretion.

If we handle a situation with a child early in the day, there is no need for our partner to get the lowdown when he or she gets home from work so another consequence can be added. Live by the slogans "No double jeopardy" and "No history lessons." The same is true for situations that arise at school: let them be handled at school. Once is enough. There is simply no good reason to bring them up with the child again.

Be sure to combine the enforcing of a consequence with warmth and support — immediately afterward if possible. We can put our arm around our child: "I know it will be hard to have to stay home after school the next two nights and miss the neighborhood fun, but I also know you are a smart kid and this will help you remember our family rule so you can be on time for dinner from now on." We can also praise our child for taking things so well. By being friendly after we hand out a consequence, we show our children it was the behavior we found unacceptable, not them. This not only reinforces the lesson; it keeps our kids from feeling unloved. In fact, it meets all three criteria for effective discipline: it teaches the desired behavior, maintains our child's self-esteem, and preserves a respectful child-parent relationship.

❧

Use stories. Storytelling and providing times of discussion are not only effective disciplinary techniques; they can also help build meaningful relationships between our children and us (discussion) and between our children and the world (story-telling). Stories also work on the subconscious level with children, so it isn't necessary to make an issue of *why* or *for whose benefit* we choose a particular story. Legends, fables, and myths often trigger insights and truths about our human nature; that's why they've survived the passage of time. For example, a child who has been having trouble telling the truth might benefit from the story of "the boy who cried 'wolf.' "

Telling our children about incidents from our own life, where we learned a lesson, or simply sharing the process by which we came to live according to the rules we do will help them develop their own moral thinking. It will help them to see that there are areas of gray, that we need to make choices in life as well as live with the outcomes of those choices, and that it is possible to be flexible in our thinking. Our trust that being a positive role model is healthier than being a dictator will benefit our children and nurture a more loving relationship with them.

It is our *attitude* that will make the greatest difference when using these techniques. If we can hold in our mind that our children are basically good, doing their best, entitled to slip up now and again, and that their behavior is not a reflection on us, and if we are well rested, well fed, enjoying life and our relationships, we will easily and spontaneously respond with one of the approaches on this list. If not, having the list tattooed on our body will not help us to remember to use it. It may take a while for our kids to get used to and respond to the new us — so don't give up.

Be patient and remember to love yourself.

Review Chapter Eleven.

Chapter Fourteen

If we accept the challenge to slow down, feel the love within us, and simply be present in the moment, we will glimpse the true joy of being a parent. If not, we risk feeling frustrated, stressed-out, and exhausted. The choice is ours — and there definitely is a choice.

The truth is always simple. When you stop and think about the various techniques and suggestions offered in *The Essence of Parenting*, aren't they simple and uncomplicated? Don't they make good sense? With the possible exception of changing our attitude about something, or modifying a belief system, everything else is relatively easy and straightforward.

Inevitably, all that really needs to change is our understanding, our perception. When we change the way we look at something, our whole experience changes. If we are open and flexible, willing to stop defending old beliefs and habits and consider new possibilities, parenting will become a joyful and effortless play. Gone will be the drudgery, the impatience, the feeling frazzled that so often characterize our daily routine.

A letter arrived recently filled with lots of questions about discipline that came up for one mom. Most of her questions seemed to be related to what she could realistically expect from her three-year-old son. She wrote, "Can I expect him to pick up his toys? Can I expect him not to whine? Can I expect him not to run in parking lots? Can I expect him not to feed grapes to his baby brother?"

By the time she finished writing the letter, she was able to see that much of her frustration — and the resulting anger —

stemmed from having unrealistic expectations for her son. It also dawned on her that working in a lab for eleven years before becoming a parent had turned her into a highly results-oriented person. She realized that a lot of her feelings about whether she was okay or whether she was having a good day were based on whether she was "getting results." Not surprisingly, she realized, she had carried this attitude into her parenting.

This mom is beginning to notice that her own thoughts and conditioned responses are more responsible for defining her experience of her son than anything inherent in him. It's exciting that she is starting to question her role in all of this, that she is asking the question, "What can I expect from my child?" After putting into practice some of what you've been reading in *The Essence of Parenting*, have you begun to notice how changing your perception even just a little opens a whole new world of experience?

Before we can relax and enjoy the thrills and chills of being a parent, it will be helpful to have a basic understanding of what we can expect from our children at each stage of development. Having just finished a chapter on discipline we expect that many people can relate to the questions asked by this mother. Typically, the subject of discipline raises a lot of questions for people. Understanding when and how to discipline our kids goes hand in hand with having realistic expectations for each stage of development.

For some of us, reviewing expectations might seem elementary or even unnecessary. Still, there are many of us who have only been guessing what *normal* or appropriate behavior looks like. Even if we think our children are beyond the ages of development we'll be addressing in the next several chapters, there is still something to be learned. We should not make the mistake of thinking that we are already beyond these years — so why bother? All of us have lived through these early stages as children and possibly as parents; so on some level we can still relate to them completely. It wouldn't be surprising if we also found an insight or two into our own adult behaviors.

છે

What can we expect from an infant? We can expect infants to sleep when they're tired, eat when they're hungry, gurgle when they're happy, coo when they're feeling playful, and cry when they need something: food, closeness, warmth, a clean diaper — or maybe just to cry. Essentially, we can expect a baby just to *be*.

Our job is to be there for our babies: to respond to their cries; to give them the food, warmth, and care they require; to offer physical closeness and warm, affectionate touch. Because infants readily absorb everything that is going on around them, they need us to create an environment that will not overtax or distress their inner state. In order to do all of this without overtaxing ourselves, we need to make sure we're taking care of our own needs.

Can we simultaneously take care of our needs and still be available to this new little person we're now responsible for? If the answer is no, what do we need to do differently to make sure this happens? Do we need to ask for help from our partner, our friends, or other people in our life willing to support us? Do we need to lower our personal expectations for daily productivity and allow ourselves time to just "be" with our baby: to leave the house a little messier, the softball or golf game unplayed, the last errand left undone?

Our lists may have to wait. Here is an undeniable opportunity to measure our ability to slow down, drop our performance expectations, see if we know how to ask for help, give and receive nurturing touch, and become aware of the support we have or haven't created in our life. This is not a gender issue. It applies equally to fathers and mothers. Watching our own inner and outer reactions when it comes to responding to or caring for an infant can tell us a lot about ourselves — possibly even how we were responded to and cared for at that age.

Our life was destined to change the moment we decided to have a baby. Were we willing to put our baby's needs ahead of our own, mindful of the care he or she would require in the early months and years? Have we accepted deep in our hearts that we are responsible for another life? Without this deep acceptance we may have difficulty changing our lifestyle or sacrificing some of the things we enjoy, like sleep, sex, time alone with our spouses, or going out with our friends. Unless we're honest with ourselves — and our spouse or partner if we have one — about our needs and our feelings, parenting an infant will feel like a burden.

A common concern of many new parents is whether it's okay to let their baby cry, especially at night. New parents are often fatigued; they feel guilty if they don't get up, but even more exhausted if they do. If your baby wakes up at night, you don't need to jump up immediately; he might simply need to fuss a bit before settling back down. Just think of your own sleeping habits: if every time you made a noise or moved someone picked you up and jostled you around, it would be pretty tough to get a good night's sleep.

Unfortunately, fatigue comes with the territory. So that we don't lose ground, we can do our best to eliminate any demands on ourselves that aren't absolutely necessary. We can rest whenever possible, take naps, go to bed early, or look for those precious moments when the baby is still, the dog is napping, and the only sound we hear in the house is the rhythm of our heart. If our mind and heart are happy, a moment of stillness may be all that's necessary to refresh the body and revitalize the spirit.

Babies as well as adults need peace at least as much as they need sleep — if not more. If our sleep gets interrupted with regularity, how we respond will make all the difference in the outcome of the experience. Agitated, angry responses will only increase the tension and add to our baby's fussiness. On the other hand, if we're able to use these interruptions to hold our child — rocking or meditating with minds filled with thoughts of gratitude and the many blessings in our life — we will both be as well off as if we had slept.

If our baby cries for a prolonged period, we can check to see if she is wet, cold, or hungry, or if he wants to be held; that much is basic. More revealing is to note our inner reaction to the crying. Do we get worried right away and start thinking the worst? Do we get resentful, angry, or impatient, feeling like it has to stop or we'll go crazy? If we know that we're too tired to get up, that the baby is okay, and that if we don't get some rest we'll be worthless to her the next day, it's okay to drop the guilt, calm our minds, and respect her need to cry. There are no hard and fast rules to follow; strive for harmony and balance instead.

A new baby can begin to set the pace for slowing our life down. We can curtail our schedules and pare down our lists if we're willing to rearrange our priorities. It is not possible to lead overscheduled, demanding lives and still be available to our children. Even though many of us try, it's just not possible to do it all and have it all. If we hope to respond lovingly and patiently to our children, to experience the joy and wonder of a new life unfolding, we will need to quiet *ourselves* more often. If we accept the challenge to slow down, feel the love within us, and simply be present in the moment, we will glimpse the true joy of being a parent. If not, we risk feeling frustrated, stressed-out, and exhausted. The choice is ours — and there definitely is a choice.

Chapter Fifteen

We know of no one who puts on a resume, "Potty-Trained at Two Years."

Hurry, hurry, hurry, no time to breathe, no time to eat. Got to get it done, so much to do, not enough time. Can't stop now, no time to waste, no time to relax. Talk to me later, see you later, I'll get to it later. No time to breathe, no time to slow down, too much to do. I'm too pooped, I'm too beat, I'm too stressed-out. No time to think, no time to feel, no time to "be." When will we slow down, if not now?

Listen to the body; listen closely. Listen to the longing of the heart for stillness. Search for the stillness that lives deep within, the stillness that supports our busy life in the world. It is there; it's always been there. Make the time. Take the time. Find it if you can. It's the true source of joy, of harmony and contentment, of peace. Peace on the inside: peace in the world.

As our babies grow, they learn to crawl, toddle, walk, and, finally, to run. Toddlers are doers and explorers. No longer confined to observing the world while on their back or sitting in an infant seat unable to move around, they learn to climb and reach and investigate. Toddlers remind us to be curious and have fun. They remind us that the world is a fascinating playground.

Since toddlers are capable of moving fast and striking quickly, they require us to remain alert and protective at all

times: losing sight of a toddler can spell disaster. So we su-
pervise our children. It is safer and easier to toddler-proof our
house than to risk injury or pick up the pieces. We can cover
electrical outlets and put sharp, hot, or expensive items out
of reach. We need patiently to divert our small children away
from untouchables over and over again — and not yell at them
or hit them. These little bundles of energy will not learn self-
discipline until at least the age of four. Our job is to provide
enough safety so Mr./Ms. Curiosity is free to explore and to
offer consistent, patient guidance when needed.

A common mistake most of us make when our children are
this age is to think that if we tell them something they should
remember it the next time. Another common mistake is thinking that if they don't, they're bad or naughty. A toddler will
unroll the toilet paper a hundred times, intentionally drop her
bowl off the high chair a hundred times, and empty the dresser
drawer a hundred times — that's the fun of toddlerhood: doing something, mastering it, and doing it again. Even their
speech reflects this: why say "Da" when you can say "Da-Da,"
"Ma" when you can say "Ma-Ma," or "Bye" when you can say
"Bye-Bye."

Let's not forget the fun of living with a toddler. What an opportunity to take delight in life, to play, to be spontaneous. Do
we delight in the play or do we see it all as work? Are we able
to support and encourage the budding curiosity and joy of dis-
covery, or are we more concerned with cleanliness and order?
Do we have a hard time playing or being playful? Are we curious about the world or bored? What do you think your own
experience of being a toddler was like?

Play. Toddlers love to play. They need to play. They learn from
play. It has been found that children learn mostly through
assimilation and accommodation. This means they learn by
adapting things to their imagination and their needs. A child
learns more by pretending a wooden block is a phone and

a cardboard box is a car than by playing with plastic replicas of the real thing. Our culture tends to promote toys that do everything for the child. When we were little we made forts out of blankets over the table. Now we can buy our kids an inflatable castle, complete with touchtone phones and microwave ovens.

So what kind of play is most beneficial? Nature provides the best toys: water, sand, soft grass; rocks and sticks and bugs that hop. Simple toys and few toys; stroller rides in the park or around the block. Fewer toys also address two of the most common complaints parents have: too much to pick up and put away, and they're *sooo* expensive. Children are more likely to learn to value and respect their possessions and will find it easier to care for their things if what they have is limited to a few basics: a ball, a doll or two, a beloved stuffed toy, a shovel and truck, some wooden blocks.

Spending time with nature is a wonderful form of play for young children. Nature gives birth to a sense of awe and wonder, attributes of a higher quality than simple curiosity. A child can be curious about how a toy truck is built, and we can show her exactly how it's put together. But can we ever fully explain how and why each bird has its own song; how and why each snowflake is unique; how and why flowers and sea shells and stones and pine cones each make a beautiful design of their own? Nature lends itself to awe, a sense that there are deeper truths than what we can see with our eyes, that there is always something beyond our senses, beyond our knowing.

The more we let our kids play spontaneously, the more creative they become at drawing on their inner resources. Play is the foundation of our intelligence, so challenging our toddlers academically before the age of five is not necessary. Their energy is better spent focused on physical development — in other words, play. Researchers have discovered that the longer a species spends in play the higher the intellectual capacity of that species. Consider the following evidence: snakes are born behaving like adult snakes; chicks spend only a few weeks acting different from adult chickens; dogs take almost a year to grow out of puppy behavior; monkeys take several years. Human beings spend the longest time in childhood — with the possible exception of the dolphin.

Some of us are in such a hurry to see our kids grow up. We want them to be able to understand and do all sorts of things; we expect them to act like little adults. We push them to hurry up and learn the skills we think are necessary to get ahead in the world. We take pride in their accomplishments and congratulate ourselves for having produced such intelligent offspring.

Children have their own innate ability. Some may read sooner than others or seem to grasp the concept of numbers more quickly. Others may seem more artistic or show promise athletically or musically. It's one thing if our children are able to do these things naturally, but to push them too early in their life because we think it's important may actually interfere with the timely development of social and emotional skills. On the other hand, some of us are so caught up in our own lives that we fail to recognize the natural development unique to our children.

Even though toddlers need to play, they aren't quite ready yet to play independently or to clean up their messes. Until they are around age five we will need cheerfully to role model those skills we wish them to acquire. We also cannot expect them to sit still for long periods, like in a shopping cart, in a high chair, in the car, or in church. If we want to be good to ourselves, we'll limit these kinds of experiences as much as possible. We may also want to consider putting limits on our visits to homes where adults are not understanding of a toddler's needs or simply do not have their homes toddler-proofed. There are times when we have no choice but to take our toddlers into situations that are going to tax both them and us. After all, we still have a life. However, we can minimize potential frustration by bringing along things that will keep our little ones occupied and by realizing and accepting that we will need to give them our attention and protection. There is a very good chance that we will not be able to sit back and enjoy whatever else is going on. For a few months out of our life, we can enjoy chasing a toddler instead.

Television. One of the hot issues in our culture is the role of television. One thing is for certain, a lot of us have relied on television to entertain and occupy our kids. We were delighted and thrilled when *Sesame Street* appeared on the scene. In homes all across America a collective sigh of relief could be heard from baby-boomer parents who were feeling guilty about plopping their youngsters in front of the tube so they could get some work done. But even *Sesame Street* is now being questioned as healthy fare for our children.

Some of us become addicted to watching television and never realize it. We like the entertainment, the companionship, the sense of connection with the rest of the world. It works its way so deeply into our lives that we never notice how it steals our time and slowly drains the intimacy from our relationships. It robs our children of hours of their own creative play, play that is good for their minds, souls, and bodies. Much of what is available on television exposes children to violence, sex, and adult behavior before they are ready to assimilate them — not that it's any good for us either. TV tries to sell us, kids included, things we don't need. We need to be aware of the impact television has on our children and make informed and conscious decisions about the role it will play in our family life. As a safe guideline, limit or delay exposure to the tube for as long as you can.

Potty-training. For both physical and emotional reasons, many toddlers are too young to be potty-trained. Their bladders are not fully developed, which in children under the age of three can lead to urinary tract and bladder infections.

Often when we start potty-training our children at too young an age, it's due to peer pressure. Once a mom in one of my classes told me that her mother-in-law insisted she had trained her son (the mom's husband) when he was seven months old — the poor baby would have had to roll to the toilet! There is no direct correlation between acceptance at Harvard and the age of potty-training. We know of no one who puts on their resume, "Potty-Trained at Two Years." We create unrealistic or impossible goals and end up frustrated, possibly yelling at or spanking our kids for not meeting *our* ungrounded expectations.

Attempting to train our children before they are physically and emotionally ready is clearly more for our benefit than for theirs. Except in highly unusual circumstances, our toddlers will come to master the art of using the toilet, and age three is not too late to start. Remember to remind them to go potty; they're not going to remember on their own. Remember to make it a pleasant experience; reward all successes.

Who among us has not witnessed our little darling crossing her knees, clutching her genital area doing the "full-bladder" dance, and still responding no when asked if she has to go to the bathroom. Accidents are going to happen from time to time until around the age of five. Kids hate to miss out on anything when they're having a good time. It's quite common for young children to get so involved in what they're doing that they ignore their bladder signals. Accidents, including bed-wetting (particularly with boys, until about age seven), are just that — accidents. So why scold or punish? A simple, "Let's clean this up; I'm sure you'll remember the next time" will suffice. Be prepared to do a lot of laundry. It takes time.

A more subtle argument against potty-training our toddlers before they are ready physically and emotionally has to do with sexuality. Consider this: are we teaching our children that someone else knows and controls their body — particularly their genitals? If yes, is it conceivable that impressionable young psyches will generalize this to mean their sexuality? Will this leave them confused later in life about whether they have the right to determine their own sexual needs? Maybe yes, maybe no; nevertheless, an interesting thought.

If we don't make potty-training a power struggle or a measure of our worth, it shouldn't be a problem. If it is or was a problem, we might want to review our attitude, feelings, and expectations in regard to this issue. They are all capable of influencing the outcome of the training. A child who experiences a lot of stress or is engaged in power struggles with an over-controlling parent may use improper elimination or holding on to their waste as a way to call attention to the problem.

People, toddlers included, need to feel some sense of personal power and control in their lives. Holding a body function hostage is not uncommon. Later in life it may take the form of an eating disorder: "Nobody can control what goes in my body except me!" If this is what's happening, scolding or punishing will be ineffective. A better option might be to seek a therapist who will not identify this solely as the child's problem, but will include the parents as well. It is almost always a two-way affair, even though we prefer to see ourselves as faultless.

If defecation problems occur much beyond age three and a half, be sure to check things out with a health professional. Some parents have had great successes with their kids' bedwetting or their bowel control problems through chiropractics. There is usually more than one way to resolve or control a problem. Ask around.

Many of us find toddlerhood the first real button-pusher in our parenting career. Our kids are starting to talk; they're developing a capacity to interact with us, and it's awfully tempting to think that they should know more and be able to handle more than is reasonable to expect at this age. Most of the time when we're experiencing stress and tension with our children, it's because of the pictures we have in our minds of what they should be like—because of *our* expectations and conditioning, not because there is something inherently wrong with them.

Having a toddler may challenge our need to have a compulsively clean house or to always put work before play. Kids this age are going to need ample opportunities for safe, healthy play and it's up to us to make sure they get them. They're going to be messy and we need to let them. More than that, we need to be able to enter into the frivolity of play ourselves and to find outlets for our own artistic expression. It's a grand opportunity for us to be young and creative again: to get down on the floor on our hands and knees, to get messy with finger paints, to sing and dance and let our imaginations run wild.

This time of life often pits the high energy, unbridled curiosity, and immense stubbornness of our toddlers against our ingrained attitudes and beliefs. The more rigid and inflexible we are, the more likely we are to suffer. The more unbending or unaccepting of what we are being called upon to sacrifice during this developmental period, the less joy we're going to experience. It can be a time filled with tension and conflict, or we can revel in the magic. How we choose to respond is entirely up to us.

Chapter Sixteen

Some of us think that our only problem with feelings is when other people lose control of theirs. Whatever the case may be, it is highly likely that our kids will end up dealing with their emotions in the same way we deal with ours.

Over the years many people have asked us if we have a particular bias. It seems like every time you turn around there is another book about parenting — ours included.

We cannot say that we are without biases; whom would we be fooling? Biases are inherent in our conditioning. However, we can say from our perspective that it's not as important which beliefs we espouse on raising children as it is how comfortable we are with those beliefs. In other words, have we found what feels right for us? Does it work?

The real issue is not what we think or believe without question — or because of how we were raised — but what we actually feel deep down, behind the voices of our parents, our teachers, the experts and the critics. Most importantly, are we able to maintain that feeling in our day-to-day life with our children? Are we able to recognize our defensiveness and judgments as reflections of our inner discontent, or do we stubbornly hold on to our beliefs, valiantly defending them even if they haven't worked for us?

Are we learning how to recognize and listen to the voice of the heart, our own ever-present inner voice? Do we see our lives becoming more light-hearted and joyful, filled with contentment and gratitude for all we've been blessed with? Is our daily experience of life changing for the better as we learn to let go of fear and resistance? Are we accepting times of struggle and frustration as opportunities for inner growth? Are we remembering to delight in the play, not to take things so seriously, and to love our children as our very own selves?

Parenting is a living process filled with infinite possibilities. It is not static where we learn something once and then never have to change our approach or our perspective. It is about each of us finding *our own* right way, a way filled with love and joy and peace of mind.

Ages two–three. In Chapter Fifteen we left off talking about toddlers. As we continue our ascent to adolescence, our focus will be on the key developmental issues many parents have asked us about over the years. As we mentioned in Chapter Five, children begin to create their own identity by acting in opposition to whatever is presented. Somewhere around the age of two or three our happy-go-lucky little charmers begin to separate from us and develop minds of their own. Typically, they become demanding and want to do things by themselves, their own way. They say "no" a lot and "mine" a lot. However, they are only doing what comes naturally at this age. There is no need to see it as a failure on our part or a challenge to our authority.

Alas, the age of sweetness gives way to the emergence of a powerful will, leaving in its wake new levels of frustration, fits of anger, and temper tantrums. So, if someone in the house — be they two, twelve, or even forty-two (we're not kidding) — fits this description, it might be helpful to reread Chapters Five and Six. Some of us may be shocked to realize that we never quite made it out of this stage of development ourselves.

Children this age are not yet mature enough to understand rules or how to share. Consequently, it is unrealistic to expect them to play cooperatively. They may play nicely on a good day, but we should be prepared for many days when they don't. A response that's usually helpful with preschoolers is, "Today Lisa just isn't ready to share her Big Wheel. Maybe tomorrow."

On the other hand, maybe Lisa won't ever want to share her Big Wheel. Every child is entitled to one or two special possessions that he or she never has to share, regardless of the circumstances.

As adults, we can try to prepare our kids for situations when they might be asked to share, praise them when they do, and help them resolve the conflict when they don't. Most importantly, instead of getting angry when our kids appear stubbornly tightfisted, we can role model how to share and then hope for the best — assuming, of course, that as adults we're capable of sharing. How do *you* feel about sharing a favorite prized possession with a friend or neighbor? I have to admit that I don't always let go freely, and I'm forty-five.

Along the same line, how do any of us feel when our children don't do particularly well playing with others? Are we quick to slip into a belittling or shaming attitude? Do we get embarrassed or feel ashamed, especially when other parents are watching? Do we take it as a personal failure? Or do we shrug it off, recognizing that *all* children go through this to one degree or another? This is another great opportunity to notice our reactions and ask ourselves why we feel the way we do.

Age four. As children move toward age four, they may have a tendency to exaggerate their feelings. In a way, they're only playing: dramatically acting out their feelings to discover what they can about them. Unfortunately, if we don't do well with our own feelings, we can expect to have problems with theirs. In fact, the exaggerated emotions of our little ones may actually cause us to feel the same unexpressed emotion in ourselves — like sympathetic vibrations. Sometimes when this happens, we try to stop our kids from expressing their feelings so we won't have to feel ours. A better option might be to make friends with our own feelings. We know from experience that many people have a difficult time with feelings; some of us realize this and some of us don't. Some of us think that our only problem with feelings occurs when other people lose control of theirs. Whatever the case may be, it is highly likely that our kids will end up dealing with their emotions in the same way we deal with ours. If we feel uncomfortable, embarrassed, or ashamed of our feelings, then that attitude and experience will be passed on to our children. If we are in the habit of ignoring, denying, or repressing our feelings, or suffering from the delusion that we have no feelings we will be unable to help our children with theirs. We cannot do for our kids what we are unable do for ourselves.

Expressing feelings is an important way to communicate if something is amiss in our life. We can help our four-year-olds learn this art of communication by helping them to identify their feelings or reflecting their feelings back to them: "You seem really angry," or "You look terribly sad." Once we've helped them gain a feeling vocabulary, we can allow them time to work through their feelings, resisting the urge to fix or smooth over whatever is creating the emotional response. Feelings are built into the system and appear whether invited or not. Some unnecessary emotional problems are actually caused by meddling in this natural process.

A child who is sad because a favorite doll is lost may cry herself a river of tears. We can offer support by acknowledging her feeling, "You're really sad that dolly's lost. I feel sad when I lose special things too." We can also suggest looking for the doll together or trusting that it will turn up. It is not helpful when we try to "fix" things by saying, "Oh, it's okay, we'll buy you a new one," or when we offer no support by denying the feeling, "Come on, that's enough crying; you have other toys."

To provide our children with the opportunity to learn how to identify and express their feelings without shame or self-judgement, we must be aware of *our* reaction to their self-expression. The more comfortable and accepting we are of our own feelings, the easier time we will have allowing them to express theirs. As a result, there will be less need to control their emotions in order for us to contain ours. And we won't be interfering with the natural process of emotional maturation.

Who can resist telling a four-year-old, "My what a big girl you're becoming?" Our kids have been busy learning, growing, and accomplishing new skills almost daily, and they deserve our praise, confidence, and recognition. However, being grown up has it's price: it's hard work. Occasionally, our four-year-olds will long to be treated like babies again. This in part contributes to the exaggeration of emotions: an unconscious attempt to get coddled again, like the good old days. Rather than reacting negatively when our "big girl" appears to regress, why not offer her some extra cuddling or rocking as we did so willingly a very short while ago. It might just ward off some whiny behavior and make a little girl very happy.

We couldn't very well talk about this developmental stage without mentioning a particularly annoying behavior of many four-year-olds: whining. The more of an issue we make it, however, the more of a problem it becomes. Our best bet is to ignore it. When that fails, having reached the end of our rope — you know what we're talking about, when their voice starts sounding like fingernails on a chalkboard — we can take a deep breath and try saying, "Could you please repeat that in a pleasant voice so I'll be able to understand you." Remember: patience, patience, patience. When all else fails, buy a Walkman.

Keeping in mind that until age five children learn mostly by following our example, we may want to take note of our own tone of voice. It could be we are the culprits, providing a lot of whining behavior for them to imitate. Ask your spouse or your friends, and be sure to tell them you really want the truth.

Besides exaggerating their feelings, four-year-olds tend to exaggerate the truth — that is, they lie. But they don't know they're lying. Four-year-olds are still so egocentric they think that if they want something to be the truth, it *is* the truth. It is all part of a "software package" that functions as a built-in "cover-your-butt": "Oh, no, I'm in trouble...I didn't do it."

Asking them, "Did you take that cookie?" is like asking them to lie.

Even if we see the misdeed with our own eyes, a four-year-old's response is likely to be the same: "I didn't do it." Instead of setting them up or, worse yet, getting into an argument about it, just tell it like it is: "You took the cookie after I told you not to. I expect you to obey me. We'll have to skip cookies after lunch today to help you remember."

Another common occurrence around this age is nightmares. As imaginations grow, some children will begin to see all sorts of creepy things in their bedroom. We may be subject to nighttime visits as active minds meet Godzilla. Or we may experience some resistance to going to bed, at least until all the suspected hiding places have been flushed out. It's a great time for dads to be heros: strong, protecting, and reassuring. Our strategy is simple: we can keep a night light on, we can escort them back to bed when fears have been calmed, or we can let them crawl into our bed for a while. In any case, this too shall pass.

To sum things up, four-year-olds are working hard physically, mentally, and emotionally; but they are still little kids who not so long ago were babies. Some days they can do it all; other days they may lose it completely. They will spill their drinks, drop their food, and make a mess. Many kids at this age continue to be — and may always be — fussy eaters. They are going to forget to brush their hair or tuck in their shirt; and from time to time may still want or need help from mom or dad to get dressed. But aren't they simply wonderful?

Chapter Seventeen

An open heart cannot live with a closed mind; love cannot flourish in an atmosphere of nonacceptance.

As our children begin to venture out, it doesn't take them long to notice that the world is filled with apparent differences. Before we know it, they're often coming back with some pretty interesting and revealing questions: "How come Sarah gets to watch TV?" "How come Jason's daddy smokes?" "Why can't we have a dog like Erin's family?" "Why does Noah's grandmother take care of him instead of his mommy?" How will we satisfy these inquisitive young minds in a way that reinforces our values and lifestyle choices without judging or criticizing someone else's?

Sometimes, a simple answer is all that's necessary: "Every family is different. We all try to do what we think is best. In our family we do such and such because we feel such and such." Putting down or criticizing how someone else lives is not only confusing to children, it speaks volumes about us while saying nothing about the other person. Judgments and criticism are bad habits that need to be broken, period. How we answer our children's questions will reveal the way we look at the world. Will we be able to guide these young minds into understanding that the world is not simply divided into good or bad, black or white, right or wrong? Will we be able to teach our children that the world is filled with infinite variety? that there are people of different races, religions, nationalities, colors, shapes, and sizes? that there are many different ways to live? Over time, our children will reflect back to us exactly how open or closed our beliefs actually are.

An open heart cannot live with a closed mind; love cannot flourish in an atmosphere of nonacceptance. The more we understand and accept apparent differences, respecting each other's values and preferences, the more love we will experience in our lives. The things we dislike or fear the most about others are also a part of us. The more we genuinely accept and respect ourselves, for better or worse, the more we will accept and respect others.

Age five. Venturing into the world may produce more than interesting questions: at times, our five- and even six-year-olds may still have trouble separating from us. When this happens, we can acknowledge their feelings with patience and empathy, fighting any temptation to dismiss them or insist that they are being silly. It is a wonderful opportunity for us to hold our kids and calm their fears. Once we've reassured them, we can then depart with our anxious ones slightly more confident that we'll be back.

Separation anxiety can appear at any time in our children's lives when they are asked to go somewhere new or leave us for a long period: overnights, camp, the first day of a new school, college, marriage! Are we ready to let go? How much of their anxiety is a reflection of our fears?

Even if we are a little reluctant to let go, some children's temperaments are such that they may always have a bit of trouble adjusting to new situations. However, a few successful experiences being away from us for short periods will probably do wonders for easing their anxiety — and ours as well.

Ages six–thirteen. Very little has been written about the years between ages six and thirteen. Maybe it's because these are the years when kids are busy being kids. Life sort of settles in and hums along. For our kids as well as us there are so many things to do, places to go, people to know: school meetings, clubs, after-school sports; homework, special projects, learning to swim; girl scouts, boy scouts, 4-H; braces, sleepovers, going to camp.

In many families, typical concerns for parents seem to be about children having either too much or not enough to do and about school performance. For kids, a lot of problems seem to be related to getting along with friends and siblings and to lack of parental involvement in their lives.

Dr. Robert Ackerman, a well-respected sociologist and researcher studying children of alcoholics, has reported that one of the major issues for young children is the parental relationship — especially in homes where there is frequent fighting, arguing, or unrelenting stress between the parents. Kids can hear and see both the spoken and the unspoken. More often than not, they lie in bed tuned into us like ham radio operators while we foolishly think they don't know or can't hear what's going on because they're asleep or because their door is closed or their room is on the other side of the house.

What children continue to need as much as ever are parents who are willing and available to listen and talk to them about their feelings, parents who take the time to get involved in their lives and include them in theirs. We must guard against slipping into the habit of going our separate ways as our kids become independent and involved in activities away from home. Independence is great, but staying connected is equally important.

Around age nine kids go through a marked developmental stage sometimes referred to as the time of "leaving the garden": something in them mysteriously "wakes up" or "tunes in," and a certain innocence is lost. "Leaving the garden" refers to the veil of childhood dropping away. Nine-year-olds seem suddenly to see the world as less than perfect; they stand in judgment, incredibly critical of everyone around them, especially their parents. Things that were once fun are now considered "dumb" or "stupid" or "boring." Nine-year-olds have been known to nitpick mercilessly at their siblings and are quite capable of being a royal pain in the rear. To keep our sanity, we can try to accept this as a stage in the development of their critical thinking skills and not take it personally. Take heart, this too shall pass.

I remember hearing about this stage of development both theoretically and from my friends whose children were going through it. Everyone warned me to be prepared for the change, but I was sure this stage would pass Hannah by. She was, after all, the most considerate, accommodating, adoring child. One day just after her ninth birthday I suggested we go for a swim and she almost snapped my head off — in the ugliest tone I'd ever heard. "Who is this child?" I thought. From that day on, for one full year, my husband and I had to grit our teeth and pray for Hannah's tenth birthday to arrive. She was so ornery we even redesigned the house we were building at the time to include an extra bedroom just for her. Ironically, by the time Hannah turned ten, the house was finished, and so was her journey to the Land of Obnoxious.

At age eleven, moodiness sets in once again, but not to the extreme of age nine. Actually, some parents notice a recurring pattern all through childhood: one easy year, one difficult year, one easy year, etc. Others observe the pattern every six months. Developmentalists attribute this all-too-familiar pattern to the stress children experience from the rapid change and growth taking place physically and emotionally. In this equation, growth means crankiness, followed by a respite: things level off for a while, stress diminishes, and then it starts over again.

In many ways this pattern seems to continue forever. All we need to do is look at our own lives, and we'll notice the same ebb and flow, the same cycles of stress followed by periods of calm. The more we are able to recognize and accept these patterns in ourselves, the easier time we will have riding out the moodiness and crankiness of our offspring. The better we are at managing stress in our everyday lives, the easier time we will have coping with their constantly fluctuating moods. Unfortunately, when our stress level gets out of hand, it's destined to clash mightily with our already moody youngsters.

Here's how it works: The laundry is piling up, the dust bunnies are everywhere, and we forgot about the meeting at school. We're tired, running late, trying to take care of one more of the endless details in our life. The car needs repair, dinner needs to be cooked, our back feels knotted, our head aches, and we're about to hit the wall. Enter our preadolescent in a funky mood. A careless remark, a little noncooperation, and the fireworks begin. What caused the fireworks? Was it really the remark, the opposition, the tone of voice? Or could it have been our own sympathetic nervous system reacting to the stress in our life, flooding us with hormones preparing us to fight? Even when we feel completely justified in our reaction there is no outside force dictating our behavior.

Conscious parenting demands constant vigilance. It requires that we pay close attention not only to our children and what's happening in their lives, but to ourselves as well. Failing to heed the obvious or subtle inner messages that flood our awareness from moment to moment — in other words, living life in an unconscious state — is usually responsible for the lion's share of our daily conflicts. As we become more practiced in the art of witnessing rather than trying to control life, the number of conflicts lessens. The more consciously we live our lives, the more we'll realize that harmony is a reflection of what's happening on the inside, not the outside.

As for relating to our children, we need to continue not only to model the behaviors we wish for them to emulate, but to support them emotionally as well. To do this effectively, we will have to be aware of and accepting of our own emotions. There's simply no other way. When our kids start riding the emotional roller coaster, we need to let them feel and experience their emotions without freaking out and squashing every outburst that rattles our cage. This does not, however, preclude us from insisting that our youngsters experience the consequences of their behaviors, emotional or otherwise. Having clear, consistent, simple rules that are reasonably easy to follow — that is, setting limits — will help make it easier to maintain healthy boundaries. Remembering to stay cheerful and positive will help to foster happy relationships.

The middle school years are about developing competency, confidence, and exploring interests. More than ever, we need to get in the game of life with our kids: support their interests, applaud their successes, empathize with their struggles. Spending time with our children is vitally important. It tangibly emphasizes that we care about them. These years are often the time when children feel the most awkward physically and socially. It's very reassuring to them to know that they are loved and accepted at home, that they can just be themselves and feel okay about who they are.

Many kids this age will struggle to maintain an outward image of being in control while at school or with their friends, only to collapse emotionally when they return home. When Jenny was in sixth grade we would hear from many of her teachers, as well as other parents, that she was such a sweet, mild-mannered, cooperative child. Lorelle and I would look at each other and wonder if they were confusing our daughter with someone else. Our experience of Jenny at home was completely the opposite: she was often surly and uncooperative and had a ferocious temper. Finally it dawned on us that Jenny needed home to be a refuge, a place where she could let off steam and still feel secure. What she needed from us was patience, tolerance, and all the love and support we could offer her. She needed us to understand.

As adolescence sets in we'll be in for a whole new round of interesting behavior. It may feel like we have a baby in our home one day, a two-year-old the next, followed by a week with a twenty-one-year-old. We need to use everything we know about caring for a one- and two-year-old when we have a thirteen- and fourteen-year-old under the roof; they are recycling the same emotional issues. Patience, patience, patience. Support, support, support. Love, love, love.

Chapter Eighteen

Learning about sexuality, embraced by the love and support of family, is as essential to our children's well-being as any other learning or training we ordinarily take for granted.

As our kids begin to explore the world outside of the family, they will also begin to explore their relationship to it. Understanding and appreciating their sexuality is an important piece of the puzzle. The earlier we are willing and able to help them with this understanding, the more prepared they will be to face the world. One of the greatest gifts we can offer our children as they begin to leave the safety and security of our homes is the self-assurance that comes from knowing and respecting themselves — physically, emotionally, and spiritually.

We know from experience that many of us have our own problems with regard to sexuality. Some of us feel sexually inadequate and undereducated, ill-equipped to be a teacher or role model. Maybe we grew up in an atmosphere where mentioning genitalia was officially (or unofficially) forbidden; and sex, if there was such a thing, was something that our parents never had. Maybe we grew up in families where we were abused, our bodies violated, and we never understood what was happening to us; all we knew was that we were scared and felt dirty and ashamed.

Talking about sex means acknowledging that our children are sexual beings and have been since the womb. It means celebrating each phase of their developing sexuality as we anticipate and celebrate other landmarks in their development like walking, talking, and learning to read. It also means ac-

135

knowledging that we are sexual beings. A healthy adult sexual relationship is the best model and teacher our children can have. Consequently, it is important to retain our sense of being a sexual partner and lover in addition to being a wife/husband or mom/dad. Children miss nothing. They know on a subtle level whether we celebrate our own sexuality, whether we love and appreciate our own as well as our partner's body.

It is a mistake on our part to assume that five- and six-year-olds are too young to learn and talk about their bodies and the nature of sex. All too soon our children are likely to have some sort of negative experience with sex: bigger kids will use rude language or tease another child; something inappropriate will be seen on TV; a magazine will inexplicably appear; or worse, they may be approached by an older child or an adult whom they know — not a stranger! Many of us have had experiences that support what we're talking about. Those of us who haven't are naive to think that it can't or won't happen. We believe that learning about sexuality, embraced by the love and support of family, is as essential to our children's well-being as any other learning or training we ordinarily take for granted.

Ideally we have already established a good foundation for teaching our youngsters about their sexuality by offering them lots of positive, nonsexual touch in their infancy and toddlerhood. They should have been given the message that their bodies are to be loved and respected and that accepting loving touch is a wonderful thing. If they haven't, it's not too late to start. Any touching that takes place now is continuing to shape our children's expectations for later in life. Whether they will expect gentle, loving touch or come to tolerate rough or abusive touch will look a lot like what we expect and tolerate in our own lives. So how about us? Do we expect to be treated with gentleness and love, or harshness and insensitivity? Do we expect to be touched at all, or have we come to expect that touch is not a part of our lives?

By this time, our kids have learned through a positive potty-training experience to listen to their bodies and respect their needs; they have also been learning how to care for and respect their bodies. Are we listening carefully to our bodies? Do we treat ourselves well? Do we love and respect our bodies and pay attention to our needs?

Another essential element in helping our kids understand and embrace their sexuality is teaching them the proper terminology. Ideally by ages five and six, our kids have learned words like "penis," "vagina," "clitoris," "breasts," and "buttocks" along with "eyes," "ears," "nose," "hands" and "feet." Ideally, they are comfortable and familiar with every part of their bodies — even though Ken and Barbie are missing important parts of theirs.

With the groundwork in place, we are ready to begin talking about sex, about where babies come from. As we become increasingly comfortable with the topic of sexuality, we'll probably notice many opportunities to ease into conversation: if we or a friend or relative become pregnant, as we see new life around us in the spring of the year, when we read stories or see pictures of babies in a book or magazine. Incidentally, this is not classified as "women's work." Fathers have many valuable insights and feelings to share with their children — daughters as well sons. Their contribution is indispensable.

Still, some of us shudder to think about exposing our children to sex at such a young age. So we wait. We wait for the day when our kids will come to us with questions even though this day may never come. In fact, most of our parents can testify that they're still waiting for us to ask those very same questions. Our children have a sixth sense about discussing sex. If we don't set the pace, they'll learn to avoid the subject. We don't have to worry about messing them up for life by accidentally giving them faulty information; any mistake can easily be corrected later by doing a little reading. It's not even necessary that we be totally relaxed and uninhibited ourselves. If we wait that long, it will probably never happen. Besides, ease and comfort come with practice. The younger our kids are when we begin, the simpler our talks and their questions will be. As they grow older and we've had more practice, we can ease into more difficult areas.

One of the advantages to starting conversations when our children are very young is that their knowledge of sex will be wrapped in the warm and wonderful feeling that comes from talking to us while cuddled up on our lap, while walking through the park hand in hand, or while laughing and looking at baby pictures in the photo album. In this way, we do what we can to nurture a positive attitude toward sexuality, to instill beautiful and loving impressions in their young hearts and minds.

Another good reason to begin talking to our children is that by age six most of them have started to figure out that if we haven't talked about sex yet, it's because sex is a taboo subject; and they will learn to withhold this part of their life from us. If this happens, we're going to miss out on myriad opportunities for spontaneous conversation: to clear up confusion, to ease fears, or to make help and support available in difficult situations. If we can talk about sex as easily as we talk about any other aspect of our life, our children will feel comfortable talking to us about any issues that come up as they grow older.

Right about now some of us are probably cringing, thinking, "Yuck, do we really have to talk about intercourse!" Why "yuck"? What kinds of personal experiences or misguided thinking — whether our own or someone else's — have created this reaction in us? Shouldn't talking about our sexuality be equated with talking about one of the most beautiful aspects of ourselves: our relationships and the expression of love and intimacy? If we don't talk about it, how and when will our children find out about intercourse: by talking to friends on a street corner or in a middle school locker room, by reading *Teen* or *Sassy* magazine or some cheesy romance novel?

I can remember being eleven or twelve years old and standing on a neighborhood corner with my friends discussing sex, a common experience in the life of a preadolescent. I was horrified when one boy claimed that his father stuck his "thing" into where his mother peed and that's how he came to be born;

most of the other boys nodded and mumbled their agreement. I remember arguing against that theory, weakly maintaining that I showed up simply because my parents wanted me to; there was no possible way my parents would ever do such a thing. I can remember feeling not only embarrassed, but stupid and somehow betrayed when I later learned the truth. I should have known. Sometimes when I recall that scene I can still feel a flush of embarrassment.

Some parents worry that their children will ask very personal questions and they either won't want to or won't know how to answer them. Yes, it could happen, especially if we've been supporting and encouraging their curiosity. Our main objective should always be to encourage our kids to talk to us about anything: "What a good question, to wonder how often daddy and mommy have sex. How often people have sex is a private matter. But some people have sex a few times a week, some a few times a month. It really depends on the people and what feels loving and right for them." The question has been answered, curiosity has been rewarded, and personal boundaries have remained intact.

Another common concern for many of us is when it is okay or not okay for our children to see us naked or follow us into the bathroom. Respecting our own as well as our children's boundaries is really the key issue when trying to model appropriate behavior or determine how much information to divulge. The best rule of thumb is to pay close attention to our level of discomfort and our children's level of discomfort and then act accordingly.

Comfort levels will vary for individual families as well as individuals within each family. Mom might always feel comfortable with her daughter in the bedroom while undressing, but will feel uneasy when her son reaches a certain age. As a rule, most children will begin to feel shy and uncomfortable around the parent of the opposite sex by about age five to seven. When this happens, we need to respect our children's feelings and ask them to leave the room while we're dressing, undressing, or bathing.

How do we know if our radar is accurate, if we are in tune enough with our children to pick up their cues? How do we know if we have good judgment about recognizing our own and our children's boundaries? We'll explore these questions in the next chapter.

Chapter Nineteen

If we pay close attention to whatever thoughts and feelings are brought to the surface as our children begin to mature sexually, we can learn a lot about ourselves.

How do we know if our limits and boundaries are healthy? After all, there is no hard and fast rule to follow, no foolproof formula that tells us if what we are doing is right. How will we know where to draw the line? What if our role modeling while we were growing up was weak, inconsistent, or outright absurd? What do we use as a measure? Recently I sat and listened to a young mother of two preschool-age children tell me about her childhood. At age twelve she was sexually molested by her uncle in a swimming pool, in broad daylight, in front of her drunken parents. For several years her mother made crude, suggestive sexual remarks about her in front of the man she was having an affair with and one night he finally tried to molest her. Fortunately, she had the strength and determination to fight him off.

Almost daily she was witness to her mother's licentious extramarital affair: in the home, in the car, in the backyard of their house. At the same time, she was witness to her father's ongoing affair with a young secretary at his office; then she would watch him coolly and unemotionally maintain his innocence when confronted at home by her mother — of all people. Needless to say, this young woman's heart and spirit were deeply wounded. Twenty years later she still feels the pain and confusion as it bubbles up into her consciousness, quite uninvited.

As sad as this story is, it is neither rare nor unique. Many people we know have lived with some sort of personal tragedy or painful episode from their past; maybe their entire early lives were a mess like in the case of this young mother. Given her experience, how is she to know what healthy boundaries are? When it comes to talking to her children about their sexuality and the nature of sex, what will she be drawing on? Memories of that time in her life still fill her with pain, anger, and even hate. One thing she knows for sure: she has every intention of giving her children a childhood different from the one she had.

Finding the love within ourselves is what makes it possible to naturally and spontaneously set healthy boundaries; and it can be our feelings that open the door to that love. When we are conscious of our feelings and allow them to be what they are without trying to hide them or deny them, we are finally able to move beyond them. Constantly pushing our feelings down or thinking we can just forget about them and get on with our life will not work in the long run. However, neither will dwelling on them or obsessing about them. When we can let ourselves experience our feelings without getting obsessed with them, we will begin to recognize ourselves as something greater than our emotions; we will begin to sense our inner essence, our inner love. From that moment on, our lives will never be the same.

Finding our inner essence, understanding that we are more than our feelings, can give us the courage we need to begin looking at past hurtful or traumatic sexual experiences. Knowing that these experiences may still be adversely affecting our self-esteem, our ability to experience intimacy and happiness, and our relationships with our children, we can listen to our own heart's prompting to take whatever steps may be necessary to heal ourselves. For healing ourselves is essential if we are to approach the subject of sex with our children openly and positively, with healthy boundaries in place. Perhaps it is time to seek counseling or, at the very least, a trusted friend to talk to or a book worth reading. Whatever the case may be, we know this can be a frightening and overwhelming undertaking. Trust your heart and know you are not alone.

Around the age of four and up we may begin to notice our kids playing doctor: "Let me see you without your clothes on"; "Let me see what this part feels like." Typically, this is a natural and innocent way for kids to begin exploring and investigating the differences they notice in one another's bodies. Still, it can be quite a shock to happen upon the scene. After we regain composure, we can use the opportunity to encourage curiosity while setting appropriate boundaries: "I see you kids are really curious about each other's bodies. That's great. But you know, our private parts are really meant to be private. So let's put our clothes back on, and maybe we can go to the library and get a book with pictures of girls' and boys' bodies that we can look at together."

Can you picture this: the lights are down low, the house is quiet, the kids are in bed, and you're in the mood for love? Through the fog of your sexual euphoria comes, "Mommy, I don't feel good. Mommy, I need a glass of water." With heart pumping and adrenaline rushing through your body, you turn over to find a pint-sized intruder peering at you with a sheepish look that says, "What are you doing?" Not only could it happen; it does happen. We simply can't be prepared for the many surprising incidents or questions that are in store for us; but our reaction to them will communicate a lot to our children.

Anger, fear, guilt, shame, embarrassment, amusement, mild annoyance — take your pick or take them all. If we live in an atmosphere where everything related to sex is secretive and shameful (my grandmother once admitted that in forty-five years of marriage she never undressed in front of my grandfather) we might scold our sleepless one or ignore the fact that he or she has witnessed our lovemaking. So what's our child going to think: that what we are doing is wrong or bad or frightening? Or worse, that he or she is bad for having done

nothing but get up to ask for a drink of water? As we become more and more comfortable with our own sexuality, we
will be in a better position to react positively, to turn those
surprise situations into wonderful learning times — times to
deepen our relationship with our children. (However, this is
an advanced form of "Parent Yoga," so good luck.)

As if playing doctor or interrupting our lovemaking isn't
enough to contend with, there's also masturbation. Many parents of preschool-age children worry that their children may
be masturbating too much. We all know (I hope) that it will
not lead to blindness, craziness, hair growing on the hands,
or sexual perversity. Masturbation is common in young children and is a natural way for them to reduce stress and nurture
themselves — and it can work that way for adults too.

If masturbation seems to be occurring in excess, it might be
a good idea to check for sources of stress overload in our children's daily life. Too much television with its constant barrage
of frenetic energy or something as innocent as a new baby in
the household are each capable of contributing to an increase
in masturbation. Children who watch a new sibling getting lots
of attention and cuddling while they are getting less may instinctively turn to masturbation as a way to calm fears about
being cast aside and replace the comfort and closeness they feel
they're losing. Instead of punishing or shaming our children
for masturbating, we can hug them and hold them and reas-
sure them that they are not forgotten, and then see what can be
done about reducing other stressors in their lives.

One of the most common fears many of us have as we wrestle
with talking to our kids about sex is what they will do with the
information. You know and we know that there's a high prob-
ability that kids — especially as they get older — will want to
share all of this interesting information with their friends. Why
not? Sex is a stimulating subject. When we talk to our kids we
can let them know that this is such a special topic that moms
and dads like to be the ones to tell their own kids about it.

Still, if our junior Dr. Ruth does decide to educate the neighborhood, at least we can be assured that she is delivering fairly accurate information. If this upsets a parent or two and we get a phone call, so be it. We can simply explain to our child, "People have different ideas about when it's okay to talk about sex, so it might be best to talk about sex with friends whose parents think the same way your mom and dad do."

Another major fear many of us have is that our children will learn about sex and want to run right out and get started. More than likely, the opposite is true. Children who get accurate information from their parents are less likely to experiment with sex than kids who don't. When kids aren't given information, experimentation becomes a convenient way to learn. Moreover, kids who aren't given information tend to lack confidence as they get older. Consequently, they are more likely to give in to peer pressure because they either don't know the facts or don't know how to make a good decision. All children will do some exploring and experimenting; it's healthy and normal. If we are willing to talk to them about sex beforehand, we increase the likelihood that they will explore safely, or at least come to us if their experimentation gets them into an uncomfortable or harmful situation.

During the middle years it is typical for girls to play with girls and boys to play with boys. Consequently, it is not uncommon for kids to continue experimenting sexually by engaging in same-sex play. They may practice kissing each other or looking at or touching each other's genitals as a means of learning more about their bodies. This can be just as shocking to happen upon as munchkins playing "doctor."

One summer day many years ago, I stepped out of the house to find my six-year-old daughter behind the bushes with a little girl from across the street. They were entwined in each other's arms and kissing each other on the mouth, oblivious to the world around them. I totally lost it. I screamed at them to stop what they were doing and sent the other little girl home. My daughter handled it much better than I did. She simply stopped what she was doing and looked at me like I was crazy. I'm also sure I said something very stupid, but fortunately I can't remember what it was. My daughter, who shall remain nameless at her request, assures me that she has no conscious recollection of the incident and I should stop worrying about it. I guess she's still handling it better than I am.

By middle school age, children's questions about sex may not only get more complicated; we may not be able to answer them all. If we're going to give our kids books about sex to supplement our ancient knowledge, we should at least make sure that the books match the stage of development our kids are currently going through. It's even better if we can take the time to read the books together. That way we can put in our own two cents by relating experiences from our childhood and also ask what things are like for them. Some kids will protest — roll their eyes and make some sort of unintelligible sound — before telling us, "It's not necessary; I already know this stuff." At this point we can tell them the review is really for our benefit to see how much we know. At the very least, let them keep the books in their room. You can bet that even the loudest protester will be up with a flashlight in the middle of the night looking at the pictures, if nothing else.

Many kids will not talk to their parents about sex, particularly if the subject has been shrouded in shame and secrecy. Still, there are times when kids need or want to talk to someone. If we've nurtured our personal relationships, ideally we have friends who will be there for our children and our children will feel comfortable going to them with their questions. If not a friend, an aunt or uncle, neighbor, clergy person, teacher, or scout leader — someone we feel comfortable asking to be there for our kids — will work just as well.

In the middle school years, kids may start using crude or "dirty" language — "swears" as it's referred to in Wisconsin. Usually, if we're straightforward about the matter, it's not a problem. That is unless we're in the habit of punctuating our own conversation with lots of "swears." It's fun to ask our kids if they know the meaning of the word they're using — which they usually don't. Many times they may be using a word just to get our attention so they can find out what it means. At this point, giving them the definition and letting them know why it's inappropriate or impolite to use it in various situations may take care of the problem. Then again, in some families, the reverse is true: our kids need to remind *us* to "clean it up."

Once when I was working with junior high kids during a silent study hall (that is, detention), a group of boys got their hands on a magazine that had an article about women's orgasms. The boys started throwing the word around, no doubt to see what kind of reaction they could get from me. I asked them if they knew what "orgasm" meant. One boy said, sure, it's a guy's dick. Another boy said, no it's not, it's that thing women get once a month — unfortunately true for many women; then again for some of us, once a month would be heaven.

They were shocked when I suggested we look the word up in the dictionary. I'm sure they never ran to get a dictionary so fast before or again. Not knowing how to spell "orgasm," they landed on the word "organism." One of the boys began reading aloud, "Any living thing that moves, grows." . . . And right on cue another piped in, "See, I told you it was a guy's dick." What a perfect reminder to lighten up and not take things so seriously.

As preparation for these adolescent years we must begin from early on to teach our children good decision-making skills. By sharing with our children what we think, how we feel, and why we do what we do, we are demonstrating what decision-making is all about. This requires rigorous, unfailing open communication. If we are honest, we will let our kids see that we don't know everything, that we make mistakes, and that as much as humanly possible we take responsibility for our actions rather than blame someone else. Above all, we must teach our children to act from their hearts.

Raising healthy adolescents requires that we approach any subject, be it sex or choosing a college, from a positive perspective. Our teenagers will face a lot of situations where they will have to make tough and important decisions. As always, sharing our lives will be the greatest teacher; ideally our children will know that they can come to us for input and encouragement to do what they feel is best. We, on the other hand, must be prepared for the inevitable times when their choices will differ from the ones we want them to make. As hard as it can be during those times, our goal should always be to instill confidence and self-respect — not fear, shame, guilt, or inhibition. When our children begin their lives without us, will they carry our blessings or our disapproval?

In the meantime, startling realities face our kids in regard to sex. One out of two fifteen- to nineteen-year-olds are sexually active. Teenage pregnancy is commonplace. AIDS is a real threat. Our young adults need to be informed! They need to know, with complete certainty, that they can come to us with their concerns and questions without fear of ridicule or condemnation. Once I ran across a list of questions that parents can give their kids to help them think through difficult decisions, for example, whether to have sex, to break curfew, or to use alcohol. It's a good list, but not meant as a replacement for honest communication between parent and child. Go through it together; offer it as a resource for times when you can't be there to talk.

1. Do I feel comfortable?

2. Do I feel pressured?

3. How would I feel if someone knew I was doing this?

4. How would I feel if a friend were doing this?

5. What could be the consequences?

6. Could I get hurt?

7. What could possibly go wrong?

8. Do the other people involved see this the same way I do?

9. Are we both (all) being honest with each other?

As a child, I had no idea what to think about sex. The one time I almost interrupted my parents in "the act," I was horrified. I ended up going back to my room feeling a strange mixture of shock and revulsion; and all I had heard through the door was the bed squeaking and a lot of heavy breathing. I grew up uninformed and hadn't the foggiest notion what role sex was supposed to play in my life. Most of my ideas came from *Playboy* or *Penthouse* magazine and standing around listening to a group of guys trying to impress each other while I pretended to know what they were talking about.

One time and one time only my father said to me, "Son, don't do anything I wouldn't do," as he was about to go out for the evening. The problem was that I didn't have the slightest idea what he wouldn't do, and I was fifteen or sixteen years old. Sad, but true.

As adults, where do we stand with our own children? Do we embrace our sexuality and look forward to sharing with our kids about the many exciting, confusing, and potentially frightening things that are in store for them as their bodies change and the hormones kick in? Or are we hoping they figure things out for themselves because this is too overwhelming for us to think about?

How do you feel after reading this chapter? Can you identify with the feelings of fear and shame in reaction to your child's budding sexuality and sexual behavior, or do you feel open and accepting of the changes? Think about your own childhood. What experiences of your own budding sexuality do you remember? Are the memories tinged with shame and embarrassment, or can you look back and chuckle, secure now in your own sexuality?

Feelings, memories, and experiences are what shape our boundaries whether we're conscious of them or not. That's what makes them worth exploring. Unfortunately, we're often not aware of what they are; that's why we keep coming back to feelings as we move from chapter to chapter. The more we understand, accept, and let ourselves experience our emotions — old as well as new — the better idea we'll have of what our personal boundaries are. It stands to reason: the clearer we are about our own boundaries, the easier it will be to help our kids establish theirs.

Becoming conscious is the precursor to change. If we pay close attention to whatever thoughts and feelings are brought to the surface as our children begin to mature sexually, we can learn a lot about ourselves. By exposing all of the negative reactions and past impressions that are consciously or unconsciously influencing our attitudes and behaviors in relation to sex, their hold on us is loosened. The more that happens, the more we are free to enjoy our own as well as our children's blossoming sexuality.

Chapter Twenty

If we were able to accept our innate goodness at every moment, no matter how we looked, felt, thought, or acted, there would be no room for guilt in our lives.

Do you have the feeling as we approach the end of the book that we've barely gotten started? It feels that way to us. Even though so many words have been written and so many ideas have been expressed, in some ways it only brings up more questions.

Recently one mother wrote: "I'm trying to accept and not judge, but I can't accept some behavior — hitting, hurting another person on purpose, unsafe behavior, etc. I want to teach my children to become responsible people. I would also like them to realize their full potential — whatever that might be. I don't know how to do those things without expecting the best from them or trying to teach them to expect the best from themselves. I guess I'm still kind of fuzzy about expectations and need some guidance. I don't want to expect too much and be judgmental and critical, but I don't want to expect too little either. And how would I really teach them to expect the best from themselves, for themselves? I don't think they need to live up to any expectations I might have, but I couldn't accept every behavior either (substance abuse, promiscuous irresponsible sex, etc.)."

For some of us, it can feel like we're constantly walking a tightrope: am I being judgmental and critical, or simply expecting good behavior? Am I helping the matter by stepping in and taking action, or is my controlling nature getting in the way again? Am I being too lenient, or is this acceptance? Always questioning, always doubting, the mind can drive us crazy with the worry game. In fact, the mind was born to play this game. The trouble is that all we get from doubt and worry is more doubt and worry. To win, we must stop playing.

Gradually, as the heart opens, our questions will fade away along with our worries and our fears. In the meantime, we can try to relax and not get so uptight about what we think our kids "should" be doing or how they "should" be behaving. Easy for us to say, you say; we don't live with your kids. That's true, we say. But the problem is not with your kids; the problem is within you.

The underlying issues raised in this letter are clearly worth considering. How do we set healthy boundaries? How do we even know what those boundaries and limits are? How do our own feelings and past experiences come into play as we try to set those boundaries? How do we deal with the guilt that inevitably comes up as we work toward finding the right balance?

Asking the questions, seeking understanding of our feelings, our attitudes, and our behaviors is not the same as worrying about them. It is a matter of opening our awareness. As we become conscious, in other words, more willing to take the time to notice what determines how we live and act in the world, we will no longer be bound by those actions. For the first time in our lives we will experience real freedom, freedom to act from our hearts and not from how we've been conditioned or programmed throughout our lives.

Why does one parent accept or tolerate abusive behavior while the partner, if there is one, doesn't even recognize it as abuse? What determines our degree of tolerance on any given day? How do we end up losing control of our children, frightened and angered by their behavior but feeling powerless to change it? Haven't we all questioned our actions and our motives at one time or another, agonizing over whether we were doing the right thing? Haven't we all experienced the ensuing guilt that comes from thinking we've harmed our children either intentionally or unintentionally or, worse, caused them to be the way they are?

We have said from the beginning of the book that taking care of ourselves, recognizing our needs and lovingly responding to them would help us to recognize and respond to our children's needs. In the same way, establishing clear and healthy boundaries, setting limits for what we will or will not accept and tolerate in our own lives will naturally result in clear and healthy boundaries for our children. Furthermore, whether these boundaries or limits have to do with behaviors or feelings, when established out of love and respect for ourselves, there can be no mistakes. When we are cognizant of what it takes to truly love and respect ourselves, when we can live our lives established in love, there will be no more questions. No matter what the situation, we will spontaneously know what to do with our kids.

Many of us think that it is selfish to take care of our own needs. We believe that we are being mean to others or irresponsible if we take care of ourselves first; or we think that others' needs, likes, and dislikes should take precedence over our own. Many of us never learned or even thought about how to listen to the wisdom of the heart, our own inner voice that constantly monitors our life and sends us messages. Instead, we have been trained from childhood to look outside of ourselves for direction and validation. Consequently, we have lived our lives focused on other people's needs and feelings while ignoring our own. In the alcohol and drug counseling field we call this "co-dependency."

We're not suggesting that we become selfish, self-centered, and self-serving, always thinking only of ourselves. This is more a matter of self-respect. If we can respond lovingly to ourselves, we will be able to lovingly respond to our children. It's that simple. If we believe our needs, our feelings, and our thoughts matter, we will know that theirs do also and act accordingly. Establishing healthy boundaries and being able to set fair, reasonable limits goes hand in hand with becoming more human, more fully our own unique, spontaneous person. When we live in accordance with our feelings, following the inner promptings of the heart, we become wonderful role models for our children.

Still, even after embarking on this process, it's not uncommon to lose our focus and begin to judge and criticize not only our children's behavior, but our own reactions as well. No sooner does our mind begin to doubt than guilt sets in: "I shouldn't have lost my temper; I should play with my kids more; I should have handled that better."

Further in the same letter the issue of guilt surfaces: "How do you deal constructively with guilt? Chapters Five and Six raised that question for me — the scene you described in Chapter Five with the mother in the park hit a little too close to home. I'm ashamed to admit how many times I've done the same thing. That leads me to guilt over the way I've treated my children in scenes like the one you described and guilt over the harm and hurt I've done to my children by acting that way."

Guilt does feel rotten, but it also feels familiar and comfortable. On a certain level, it helps us maintain a sense that deep down we are nice people. After all, we may do rotten things, but at least we feel "good and guilty" about it; if we didn't care, we wouldn't suffer so.

We think, for whatever reason, that things have to look a certain way or be "perfect." We're horrified when we make mistakes. Fearing the criticism of those both real and imagined, we become frustrated, angry, and ashamed when we don't measure up to our unbending standards of perfection. If, on the other hand, we were able to accept our innate goodness at every moment, no matter how we looked, felt, thought, or acted, there would be no room for guilt in our lives. We are in the habit of feeling guilty, and some of us can't break the habit.

We love swimming around in the juicy melodrama of our worries and guilt. For some of us guilt is more than a habit; it's an addiction. It seems incredible, doesn't it, that we would be so attached to something that feels so awful and serves no purpose? The solution is simple, but not so easy to do: change the direction of our thoughts.

"But if we don't feel guilty, how will we ever change? We'll always be rotten parents screaming at our kids. It's not possible to live a responsible life without guilt." Says who? Once we understand what we're doing to ourselves, why continue to do it? Why habitually reinforce patterns of thinking and feeling that make us feel rotten and reinforce our false ideas and doubts about ourselves? Most of us have spent twenty, thirty, or forty odd years digging a guilt trench one thought at a time, that's why. It has to stop!

We can begin to eliminate the habit by first replacing and then dropping any thoughts that lead to feeling guilty. However, before we can replace these thoughts or eliminate them, we have to catch them. This requires slowing our lives down enough to watch what's going on in our minds. We are not our thoughts but the witness of our thoughts. The witness forms no opinions, judgments, or criticism about what it sees; it's simply that part of us that knows what we're thinking. The more diligently we practice being the witness, the easier it will be to identify and ultimately replace or let go of unwanted thoughts.

Put the book down and close your eyes. Imagine yourself sitting alone in a dark movie theater gazing intently at the screen. All your thoughts, feelings, and physical sensations are the feature presentation. Watch them come and go as if you were watching scenes from a movie. If you get captivated by a particular story line or overidentify with a feeling or sensation, remind yourself that it's just a movie. You are not in the movie, you are the observer, the one sitting in the theater watching. The more we are able to identify with the witness, our true Self, the less affected we will be by the content of our thoughts. The less affected we are, the easier it will be to replace them or let them go.

Still, getting rid of guilt can be tricky. If we become too serious about the process we may unintentionally fall right back into feeling guilty: "Oh, no, I'm having a guilt thought; I'm not supposed to do that. I'm so rotten; I should think something positive. I'm so bad at this; what can I think that is positive? There's nothing positive about myself." Guilt, guilt, and more guilt. We're really not so bad, you know; we're just in the habit of thinking we are. When we see a guilt thought, we can immediately replace it with a positive one. If you can't think of anything positive, try a ridiculous thought, a joke, or a silly song — whatever it takes to break the habit.

In my own struggle to break the guilt habit, one thing I found particularly helpful was to contemplate this metaphor: Our thoughts are like leaves on the trees, beautiful and fascinating in form and color. (In Wisconsin that takes on even more meaning in the fall, which was when I was working with this concept.) But like the leaves at summer's end that shrivel and fall away, only to be replaced in spring by another set, our thoughts also come and go.

We can spend our lives strongly identified with the leaves (our thoughts) and define our existence by them — glorious at times, rotting at others. Or we can become identified with the sap that runs through the trunk of the tree (our inner essence), the life force that exists before and after the leaves are gone, the life force that will take new form even after the tree no longer exists.

With this picture in my mind, every time my thoughts would begin to dance and spin, weaving their captivating web, I would imagine leaves falling from a tree and simply let them go. As I watched the leaves slowly drifting to the ground, my awareness would turn to the life force running through the trunk and branches of the tree, the life force that gives rise to all existence, our innermost Self. In no time at all, expansive, relaxed, and joyful feelings would replace the murky mood my thoughts had created.

So what does all of this have to do with boundaries and our kids? If worry, fear, doubt, and guilt are eliminated from our repertoire, if our mind and heart are still and focused on the truth, we can trust that any response we have to a given situation will be appropriate in that moment. Certainly an open heart and steady mind will instinctively know how to respond to any situation. When we take worry and control out of picture, many more options become spontaneously available to us. Depending on circumstances, the moment, the people involved, we might respond quickly and directly or slowly and subtly. We might be firm and unbending, gentle and flexible, or anything in between. Doesn't the same rich and fertile soil give rise to an infinite variety of life?

There is much, much more that can be said about establishing healthy boundaries, setting limits and dealing with guilt. For now, it's time to practice what we already know: guilt and worry have to go! A treasure house of love and joy lies patiently waiting to be discovered. Find the witness and you find what you've been seeking.

Chapter Twenty-One

Setting healthy boundaries starts and ends with loving our-selves. We must become spiritual warriors: guardians of the inner treasure, our rightful inheritance, love.

Letting go of guilt will happen naturally when we are firmly rooted in self-love and acceptance. Healthy boundaries will arise spontaneously out of self-respect. The path is narrow and hard to follow. One day it's all so clear and the next day we're in a fog. Our feelings open the door and the next moment they're leading us away from the truth. We need to think before we act, yet too much thinking and we're lost. The mind struggles to understand, yet understanding alone is not enough.

Having healthy boundaries is not something we do; it's a way of life. It's about taking responsibility for our own well-being and safety. It's about being willing to provide for ourselves all that we need physically, emotionally, and spiritually — when we need it. It's about giving ourselves the opportunity to feel our feelings, accepting them without judgment and expressing them in ways that will not harm ourselves or others. It's know-ing that there is no one else to blame for our feelings. If we're frustrated or irritated, angry, sad, lonely, or hurt, it's up to us to recognize what we need to move through and beyond those feelings: a change of heart, more rest, honest communication, asking someone to change his or her behavior, or perhaps just acknowledging the feeling and letting it be on its way.

In my own life I've found that setting boundaries requires constant vigilance. While I'm usually more than willing to go the extra mile for my children, spouse, and friends, I often cut corners when it comes to myself. I realized once that the way I set boundaries was to make sure everyone else got what they needed first before squeezing out a little something for myself. I had convinced myself that this was what a "good" parent did. Was I wrong! Living that way had made me incredibly susceptible to burn-out, fatigue, depression, and irritability. All I had really done was cultivate a horrendously ugly inner space, and that's what we draw upon to nurture our families.

Since then, I've learned that I must continually evaluate how I take care of myself. Sometimes, when I want to get a clearer picture, I step out of the personal experience and objectify the situation: I look at how I'm living, at what I'm allowing in my life, and ask myself, "Is this the life I want for my children?" Do I want my kids skipping meals or having no playtime? Do I want them suffering under the weight of self-criticism and harsh judgments, constantly berating themselves for making mistakes? Do I want them feeling responsible for taking care of everyone else before they take care of themselves, or to have such high expectations they will never be able to meet them? Once I'm clear about how I've been treating myself, I'm better able to make whatever adjustments are necessary to become more consistently loving, nurturing, and self-protective.

Sometimes being self-protective means setting limits with those we live with — for instance, our children. There are definitely times when we're going to need a break from our kids, or at least from their whining and fighting. From the perspective of taking care of ourselves, we might have to tell them they need to leave the room or that we need to leave the room and don't want to be disturbed for a while. If we have a colicky infant or a high energy two-year-old and can't leave them alone, we can ask a friend or our spouse to take over periodically, or we can hire a baby sitter and give ourselves a break.

We are all capable of making these choices. Finding excuses merely indicates our reluctance to take responsibility for ourselves. But maybe we like playing the martyr, maybe we're hopelessly attached to our misery, or perhaps nobody ever told us we had a choice and we simply need to find out for ourselves that it's not being selfish. As we experience this reality — that caring for our inner state will produce a more satisfying life — we will find the courage and confidence to consistently take care of our needs. We might even come to like it.

Taking care of ourselves looks, sounds, and feels a whole lot different from blaming others for how we feel. Rather than, "You kids are so inconsiderate, I can't stand it any more, get out of here!" it begins to sound more like, "I'm tired and irritable, you kids need to go in another room with that game."

When we truly believe that we are worth taking care of and that we have the right as well as the responsibility to take care of ourselves, we will be able to express our needs confidently without a lot of yelling, complaining, or excuses. Usually we yell and offer excuses because we haven't convinced *ourselves* yet that what we are doing is okay. We often feel guilty about taking care of ourselves. When we're yelling at our kids or spouse, we're only trying to get ourselves to listen.

The closer we can come to expressing our needs without the yelling and the excuses, the more likely people will respect our limits. It is the conviction, the certainty in our voice — not the volume — that people respond to. When we are no longer using up our energy trying to convince ourselves we mean business, people will instinctively know it. They will also know we mean business when we follow through. Remember those kids we asked to leave the room? If they don't leave after one request we need to escort them out. Imagine their surprise when our words turn into action. That's making sure we are taking care of ourselves. That's being consistent and self-disciplined. That's setting healthy boundaries.

Children and adults will respect us and feel more comfortable around us when our boundaries are clear. When they're not clear, our reactions are often erratic and murky, reflective

more of our mood at the moment than a consistently identified boundary. People never know what to expect: one time
we're tolerant and the next time we're on the warpath. They
never know when they are overstepping our limits and when
they are not. When people don't know where they stand, or
how far they can go, they usually end up either avoiding
us because of our unpredictable explosiveness or manipulating us because they know we won't follow through. Children,
spouses, friends, and co-workers may actually think *they* are
the ones responsible for our mood, and not us. But they aren't
any more responsible for creating our mood than we are for
creating theirs. Think about it.

At first we may need to do some yelling to set limits, especially if that's the only way people take us seriously. It's okay.
What's important is to begin setting limits. If we have doubts
about what we're doing, people will only hear our doubts. If we
ourselves don't really believe what we're saying, others won't
believe it either. Remember, it's not the volume people respond
to, but the unwavering conviction they hear in our voice.

As we begin to listen to ourselves more frequently, paying
close attention to our subtle feelings, we will find ourselves
yelling less. Slowly and steadily we will make the shift away
from thinking we have to manage, fix, or control other people's
behaviors in order for us to feel okay. In time, as we experience
ourselves becoming loving self-caretakers, most of the tension
and conflicts that used to visit us on a daily basis will simply
disappear. Peace and harmony will be achieved through inner
transformation, not outer control.

The best way I've found to avert yelling is *prevention*. Since
most of us are way too self-sacrificing for our own good, we
may need to be extremely generous, almost lavish with ourselves when we enter into the unfamiliar world of self-care. In
other words, we must not leave *anything* out. Forgetting to care
for ourselves is another habit that needs to be broken. Protect

your quiet time, playtime, mealtime, and exercise time dili-gently. Reward yourself often for all your hard work: a regular warm bath, a night out, a good book, a massage, lunch with a friend, a day on the golf course.

Over the years, I've discovered several warning signs that faithfully tell me when I'm losing sight of my boundaries: feel-ing like I do more than anyone else, feeling unappreciated, feeling like I want to withhold my love until someone else showers me with theirs, being critical of others for not doing everything I think they should be doing. When I see ingrat-itude, insensitivity, or ineptness in others I'm seeing those qualities mirrored back to me. As much as I would love to be-lieve my critical eye is unerring or that I possess the gift of accurately analyzing everyone else's behavior, what I see are only reflections of my inner discontent — bits of poison waiting to be flushed from my system. No matter how hard I wish at times it wasn't true, I can see in others only what exists in me.

The poison that eats away at my peace of mind is forgetting to love and care for myself, thinking that I am undeserving or unworthy of love simply because I exist, not because I did something to earn it. Whenever I start feeling this way — the result of not having set limits that protect my inner sense of well-being — there's no doubt that something is amiss in my life. The feelings are right there in front of me, impossible to ignore; everything around me starts to fall apart. Yet once I'm able to recognize what's happening, I know it's only a re-minder to turn my attention inside; and there without fail is the guilt, doubt, fear, or self-neglect that got the whole scene started. I know now these feelings are red flags telling me to slow down and offer *myself* what's missing in my life: love, tenderness, respect, and acceptance.

Not too long ago I had a weekend to myself while my spouse and kids went camping. I used the time to write, walk the dog, do some housework. On Sunday, to welcome everyone home, I decided to fix a big turkey dinner. When they finally returned,

I encouraged them to rest and take warm baths while I did the unpacking and got the dinner on the table. Afterward I cleaned up while everyone but me relaxed in front of the television. When I finally had a chance to sit down, I had a pile of laundry to fold and mending to attend to. I never even got around to the quilting I had hoped to do. By the time I went to bed, I was exhausted and disappointed.

I felt like no one really noticed how hard I had worked, how I had sacrificed for them. I felt unappreciated and abandoned by my family. I was so hurt and angry I couldn't respond to my spouse's invitation to be close in bed. As my despair and anguish intensified, I started to list in my mind all the things I *do* and all the things my husband *doesn't* do. I was boiling mad. After staring at the ceiling for two hours and refusing to talk because I hated myself for being such a witch, I finally blurted it all out — and of course hated myself even more. After all, I have such a wonderfully supportive spouse; how could I be such a nag?

It wasn't until the next day that I was able to step back and see where I had let my limits slide. It was obvious from all the yelling and the depression that followed — ruining by the way what could have been a night of romance — that I had lost touch with my needs. But it wasn't so obvious the day before, when I had neglected to monitor the thoughts, feelings, and motivations behind my actions.

Why did I think I had to work the whole time everyone was gone? Why did I have to fix the big meal? Why didn't I forget about cleaning up and packing the next day's lunches and jump on the couch and relax with everyone else? Why didn't I leave the sewing and folding for another day? Why was I so driven?

Deep down I wasn't feeling *worthy* of being loved or appreciated. Deep down I felt I would be a better person and therefore more deserving of love and admiration if I did all those things. I wasn't content just to please myself. That poison that says, "If I want love I have to earn it; it's not enough to be loved because I'm me," had bubbled up from my subconscious. Seduced by the power of those deeply rooted feelings, I wasn't able to stop, to feel satisfied with how much I had done. Cooking the dinner was fun, but why hadn't I said to myself, "Wow, what a great meal; you deserve a break; take a load off; relax for the rest of the night"? Something inside believed I didn't *deserve* to have time off. I felt guilty about having had a little time to myself so I made up for it by working overtime when the troops got home. As if that wasn't enough, I blamed everyone around me for the way I felt.

It is so much easier to think we can fix others than it is to let go of external circumstances and take care of ourselves. As long as we believe someone else is causing us to feel what we feel, we're likely to waste our energy trying to fix, change, or control them so we'll feel better. Without realizing it, we'll be perpetuating the very conditions in our lives we're trying to eliminate. The more we try to control things externally, the more we'll end up infringing on other people's freedom to be themselves. When we finally get it — that what's happening in the outside is only a mirror of what's happening on the inside — we'll realize that there's no one to change but ourselves and that how we feel at any moment, about anything, is not dictated by outer circumstances, but by our own inner state. Setting healthy boundaries starts and ends with loving ourselves. We must be faithful in offering ourselves what we need. We must be constantly on the alert for old, familiar feelings that bubble up into our consciousness, ensnaring us and holding us captive. Facing our demons will be scary at times, exhilarating at others. We must become spiritual warriors: guardians of the inner treasure, our rightful inheritance, love.

Chapter Twenty-Two

Taking care of ourselves, responding to our own needs with love, is what makes it possible to be the kind of parent we dream of being. Self-discipline is indispensable. It is the path to freedom, a key that unlocks the treasure of the heart.

Life is such an incredible play. In the last year, children have grown, relatives have died, babies have been born, jobs have changed, houses have been sold, illnesses have come and gone. Try as we might to control it, life seems to have its own rhythm. The great teachers, the spiritual masters, tell us that the only thing that never changes is our inner Self — the silent witness. The more we become established in *witness consciousness*, the more love and harmony will be manifest in our lives. Why? Because love and harmony are attributes of that state. Living with this awareness is the key to happiness, to mastery of our life, to the essence of parenting.

In our introduction we encouraged everyone to read each chapter more than once: the more often you read the chapters and consistently put into practice what is being offered, the more growth you will experience in your life. Self-discipline, practice, patience, and a sense of humor — remember?

Have you been remembering to make self-discipline a part of your everyday life? Human nature being what it is, self-discipline is generally not high on our list. Therefore it must be faithfully cultivated and nurtured if we are to experience its many blessings.

How does one go about cultivating and nurturing self-discipline? To begin with, by recognizing its true value. Without discipline our minds have a tendency to run wild. Without discipline our feelings are apt to run amuck. There is an old expression in counseling: feelings follow thoughts. Without discipline we are quite helpless against the myriad thoughts — and subsequently feelings — that would otherwise rule our lives. So much of our unhappiness, our discontent, impatience, intolerance, anxiety, fear, criticism, and judgments have their origins in an undisciplined mind.

Self-discipline is knowing and remembering our own value and worth when every cell in our bodies is believing otherwise. It requires the willingness, the strength and fortitude, to pick ourselves up and keep going when all we want to do is give up, when our minds are screaming, "Enough, enough, I can't stand it anymore!" Self-discipline is having faith in the knowledge that we are good people; we work hard; we deserve to be happy. It is knowing that any thoughts or beliefs to the contrary are self-defeating, demoralizing, and only lead us away from the truth. True self-discipline is recognizing how quickly and easily our own thoughts steal our happiness and throw our lives into disarray.

All of us make mistakes. We all end up feeling guilty about one thing or another. Self-discipline is the willingness to accept our own shortcomings and failures. It is the gentle touch of forgiveness when we're screaming for retribution. It is knowing that our anger, the poison pumping through our system, the feeling we're about to unload on our children or spouses or friends or co-workers, is ours and ours alone. Self-discipline is remembering that there is no one to blame; there is no one making us feel the way we do; there is only our own anger. It's knowing at those times when we're pointing the finger, drowning in self-righteousness ready to condemn, that it's all a play of consciousness. Who are we really angry at? Why are we so hurt? Who is the one burning with these feelings?

Self-discipline arises out of faith and conviction. We do not achieve it through rigid enforcement of our beliefs and opinions. It is not about forcing ourselves into austerity or walking around thinking we can't have fun until the work is done. It is also not about ignoring or denying our feelings because we think it's a virtue not to be scared or angry or hurt. Self-discipline is about remembering the truth when our minds are filled with doubts. It is the willingness to reach again and again and again for the love and compassion, the gentleness and kindness that lives within our heart.

"It sounds good, but I just don't have the time right now" is a theme familiar to many of us. It's true, our lives are extremely busy; and everything does seem to be happening faster. Yesterday my daughter was in second grade; now she is in college. So many things to do, so many places to go, so many decisions — it hardly seems possible to take the time to sit and be still; and many of us don't. Yet if we are not willing to embrace this practice, we are destined to end up living our lives like a dog chasing its tail: chasing happiness, chasing contentment, chasing love and never quite catching up.

Throughout the book we asked many questions. Some of them appeared simple and straightforward: What have you noticed about your predominant feelings lately? When you closed your eyes did your mind run wild? Have you ever caught yourself sounding like a drill sergeant? Others appeared more involved: When and how do we come to distrust our own feelings? When do we stop living life spontaneously when it started out being so natural? If we get hooked in a struggle and find ourselves overreacting in word and action, what in us is reacting so strongly?

What all the questions had in common was their ability to reveal something about ourselves. Even a simple question, one that we could easily have taken for granted, had the potential to unravel the mystery of who we are and how we live our lives. The only important variable in this process was whether we took the time to consider it. Were we willing to really ask ourselves the question or did we shoot right by it?

Were you really going to stop reading for a moment and actually consider the question, or were you about to shoot right by it? Be honest. Aren't we all somewhat guilty of merely agreeing intellectually with something because it sounds familiar or disagreeing with it because it doesn't readily fit our own ideas or beliefs? Don't we often, in the course of daily living, shoot right by something because we either don't recognize its true worth or don't want to take the time to stop what we're doing?

In our opinion, it's epidemic. Call it a sign of the times; call it the nineties; time is flying. A while ago we met with a woman who produces a resource guide for mothers. Although her main objective in meeting with us was to sell advertising space, she had on an earlier occasion solicited an article from us for publication in her periodical. With great excitement we handed her a short article written in the spirit of the book that used some material from one of the chapters. She skimmed over it briefly and then in a very patronizing way said, "Can I be honest with you? This is too touchy-feely for my readers. Besides, when you've been in the business longer, you'll realize that people are looking for fast answers; they want it short and simple; they don't have time and they don't want to have to work for it."

After the meeting we wondered how long someone would have to be in the business; we already had over thirty years between us and that didn't seem to be enough. We're not from another planet. We know very well how busy life can be; we are both working and raising families. Indeed we also know the temptation to seek out fast answers or rely on shortcuts; time is as precious to us as it is to anyone. However, this is not simply an issue of time management. What we're talking about is living and parenting consciously. Shortcuts and fast answers can be useful. They can also be a problem if they are seen as the goal and not simply a way to make our lives easier. In fact, being busy is a problem only if it distracts us from the truth.

Parenting consciously is compatible with living a full and rich life. The spiritual masters demonstrate time and time again that being busy is not an obstacle on the spiritual path. Why should it be an obstacle in parenting? They teach that mastery of our lives begins with recognizing the truth behind our thoughts and feelings, behind our beliefs. If we can learn to live and parent consciously — nurtured by the unlimited love and wisdom that supports all life — we will no longer be overwhelmed by the constant bombardment of endless details that plague us daily. When we finally *know* deep within our hearts that there are no limits to what we can accomplish but those we impose upon ourselves, our lives, let alone our parenting, will become an effortless play.

Not only will our parenting become more joyful and spontaneous, the very quality of our lives will begin to reflect the nature of this state of being. This is neither idle fancy nor idealism. Our inner essence is already loving and compassionate, nurturing and supportive, gentle and kind; these attributes are already ours in full measure. Becoming conscious of our true worth, loving and respecting the truth that lives within our heart, is what makes it possible to do the same with others. Knowing that these qualities exist, that we were not in the rest room when they were being handed out, is the first step to manifesting them in our lives.

Love, compassion, gentleness, kindness, sensitivity — without them our lives are like a flower without scent or food without taste. Yet, that's exactly how many of us live. Instead of savoring and delighting in the richness of our life, we moan and complain about how much we have to do. The more stressed-out and exhausted we allow ourselves to become, the easier it is to forget the truth.

Taking care of ourselves is so basic to living a happy, balanced life, it's a marvel that so many of us are unable to do it. Did our parents forget to tell us about this? Is this a variation on the concept: "suffering leads to salvation"? It doesn't take a genius to figure out that stress and exhaustion do not lead to kindness and sensitivity. In the same way, love and compassion will not flourish in an atmosphere of fear, anger, tension, and anxiety.

Much of *The Essence of Parenting* has stressed the need to take care of ourselves, to seek a more natural, spontaneous direction in our parenting and our lives. This is not an invitation to drop our responsibilities. Nor is it the "me-generation" of the sixties revisited. It is an invitation to find the balance between taking care of business and taking care of ourselves. The key word here is "balance." Trying to live a busy life without taking care of ourselves can only lead to frustration, irritability, and burn-out. Taking care of ourselves, responding to our own needs with love is what makes it possible to be the kind of parent we dream of being. Self-discipline is indispensable. It is a path to freedom, a key that unlocks the treasure of the heart.

Chapter Twenty-Three

Remembering the truth of who we are inside, loving and respecting the greatness of our human heart, is what makes it possible to maintain the balance between grace and self-effort, between responsibility for others and responsibility to ourselves.

Every time we set eyes upon our children we gaze into the mirror of our life. Every day we are given the opportunity to learn patience, humility, and flexibility; to bring joy and humor, gentleness and kindness, love and compassion into the world. Every day we are given the choice of how we are going to live our lives, of how we are going to treat others, of how we are going to treat ourselves. How is this possible if not for grace?

It seems fitting as we bring this book to an end that we acknowledge the role of grace in our lives — not to belabor a point, but out of heartfelt gratitude for the privilege of being a parent, of being able to watch and participate in the growth and development of our children. How can we not be grateful when every day we take part in the miracle of another life unfolding?

Remembering the truth of who we are inside, loving and respecting the greatness of our human heart, is what makes it possible to maintain the balance between grace and self-effort, between responsibility for others and responsibility to ourselves. What is this balance between grace and self-effort, between responsibility for others and responsibility to ourselves?

As parents, most of us are well aware of effort. From the

171

moment our children were born our lives became more complicated: needs changed, routines changed, schedules changed; our responsibilities increased dramatically. The only thing that didn't change was the number of hours in a day. Effort we understand.

If we live superficially, worried only about how we look or what others think, our lives may appear clean and orderly, attractive on the outside, but lack a certain depth of feeling or purpose. We may find ourselves consciously or unconsciously choosing style over substance. But style will not produce the love and joy we are seeking in life. If all our effort goes into looking good, into keeping up with the neighbors, acquiring a bigger this or a better that, what is left to search for meaning or truth? Our kids may very well end up living in a beautiful house, dressed in beautiful clothes, thinking this is what life is all about.

The essence of parenting has a great deal to do with where we place our efforts. Making the effort to become conscious, to increase our awareness, to open our hearts is what will bring meaning and substance to our lives. Living in a way that brings us closer to the truth, that leads to lightheartedness, honesty, generosity, playfulness, and a steady mind is the essence of self-effort.

Improving ourselves, freeing ourselves from the debilitating effects of incessant negative thinking, judgments, and criticism, eliminating the barriers that separate us from our loved ones demonstrate self-effort. Turning ourselves in the direction of love when our whole being is crying out in rage or blame, reaching for forgiveness when we've been hurt, letting go of resentments, fighting off depression — these are the heart of self-effort. Can we live without doing these things? Of course we can. It's just that turning ourselves in the direction of love is what brings more love into our lives; embracing forgiveness, letting go of resentments, and rising out of despair are what open the heart and make room for grace.

❧

When we are dealing with grace the picture gets a little fuzzier. We may have a vague idea of what the "grace" means, but typically it's not a term that we toss about in our everyday conversation. Yet ironically without grace there would be no picture. We are alive because of grace. We are who we are because of grace. Grace is the guiding force in our lives. It is the urge to reproduce, the love for our children, the strength to leave an abusive relationship. Grace brings us out of bed in the morning and moves us through the day. It steels us in the face of adversity and softens us when the trial is over. It is what moved us to write this book and you to read it.

Grace is what makes it possible for our mind to think, our heart to pump blood, our intellect to discern the truth. It is the source of inspiration, the tug on our conscience, the light in our eyes. Grace is always present in our lives. It is the force behind all of our actions. It is our unfailing support in the world. To feel its touch we have only to open our minds and our hearts and embrace its presence.

Living our lives unaware of grace is what makes effort feel like a burden. We all know full well that without effort, nothing gets done: the laundry piles up, the dishes go unwashed, the bills remain unpaid. Have you ever tried not doing anything, crossing your arms and deciding you're through, you've done enough? None of us can do that for very long. Sooner or later we'll have to go the bathroom; sooner or later we're going to get hungry; sooner or later the very force of our lives will pick us up and get us moving again. Effort happens with or without our participation; it is part of life. But does it have to feel like a burden?

Overcoming adversity, meeting challenges, coordinating a mountain of details, striving for harmony against the forces of chaos are the cornerstone of parenting. How we approach this Herculean task — our frame of mind, our understanding, our feelings about what we are doing — is what determines our experience every day of our lives. Do we embrace parenting with a light heart, a steady mind, and a sense of connection to something far greater than ourselves, or do we wear ourselves out constantly feeling like we're struggling against forces beyond our control?

Raising a family can at times feel overwhelming: fear, anger, loneliness, frustration, anxiety, doubt, depression — all seem to come with the territory. We have all experienced the struggle. How we handle these times of struggle, not whether we'll experience them, is the essence of parenting. We can feel disappointed, angry, hurt, or afraid, yet striking out at others only perpetuates the feeling. Overcoming or letting go of these feelings takes effort, yet it happens through grace. How long we stay angry is up to us. Whether we allow fear to rule our lives is up to us. What we think, what we choose to believe, is also up to us. We have the power to turn ourselves in any direction, to control our minds, to master our emotions.

A light heart and a steady mind do not come easily. And they are not cheap. They are born out of the constant practice of self-discipline. The ability to live our lives without being beaten down, to perform our tasks, to meet our obligations and responsibilities with love and compassion rather than harshness, pettiness, selfishness, and resentment is the result of the balance between self-effort and grace. We are supported by grace; it happens through grace; yet it requires self-effort. We must make the effort, yet grace performs and supports the effort. We must act, yet the strength to act comes from grace.

Through grace and self-effort our relationships with our children, our spouses, and our friends begin to reflect the wonders of the heart. Whenever we make even the slightest effort, the slightest adjustment in our attitude, we will feel the touch of grace in our lives: love and joy, affection, intimacy, patience and tolerance — all will spontaneously bubble up from within.

Early in the book we asked: If we find it difficult to take care of ourselves so that we're not living a healthy, balanced life, how can we have this expectation for our children? Haven't you noticed that the more care we take to protect our well-being, our peace of mind, and our physical strength, the better able we are to take care of others? Assuming responsibility for others, be it children, spouses, or older parents, when we are unwilling to take care of ourselves, is an empty practice. It seems pretty obvious that ignoring our own needs for the sake of others isn't a very satisfying way to live. Burning the candle at both ends, sacrificing unnecessarily for our children, spouses, employers, or anyone else, neither ennobles us nor leads to happiness and contentment. On the contrary, it makes martyrs out of us; and who wants to live with a martyr?

When we get worn-out and run-down, aren't our patience and tolerance the first things to go? Aren't we harder to live with? But when we take care of ourselves we are in the best shape to take care of others. So why do so many of us nod our heads in agreement and then go through the day not taking the time to eat properly, exercise, or rest? We insist that our children — especially when they're younger — eat a balanced diet, take naps, and have sufficient play time and quiet time. But when it comes to ourselves, the rules no longer apply. Instead, we choose to live with constant stress, even exhaustion, telling ourselves that we don't have time to slow down, there are too many things to do, so many people depending on us.

Remembering our true worth as persons, remembering what lives within our heart — in other words, practicing self-discipline — will lead to greater self-respect. In time we will find ourselves paying closer attention to our own needs. We will no longer want to push our bodies to the breaking point, or go without proper nutrition, or live with the stress of painful emotions. Out of a growing love and respect for ourselves, it will become easier and more natural to care for others. As we learn to respect ourselves, we will naturally respect others; as we practice taking better care of ourselves, we will automatically take better care of others. This is maintaining the balance between responsibility for others and responsibility to ourselves. It happens through grace; yet it requires self-effort.

We have stressed the need to take care of ourselves, to seek a more natural, spontaneous direction in our parenting and our lives. Unfortunately, this is not as simple as it sounds. Sometimes it feels so much easier just to keep living the way we've been living; and make no mistake, that is always a choice. None of what we're talking about happens without a great deal of effort and sacrifice. Changing our thinking, our beliefs, or our approach to life is a tall order. What makes it worth the effort is that any change for the better, any lightening of our inner state, any opening of our heart produces tangible results. Our children will know. Our spouses will know. Our friends and co-workers will know. And best of all, we'll know.

Harmony and contentment are not mythical concepts; they are the result of being willing again and again and again — when tired, frustrated, depressed, or disillusioned — to remember what's important, to remember who we are and what life is really all about. If you've been trying conscientiously to incorporate some of the concepts we've been talking about in *The Essence of Parenting* into your life and you're still not getting the results you would like, keep practicing and have faith. It's not easy and it doesn't happen overnight.

These concepts are a direction we can take in our life, something to strive for — if we want to. Practice, commitment and devotion will not fail us. Whatever happens along the way, resist the urge to feel guilty: "I'm not working hard enough"; "I just can't get it right"; "I must have been absent when they were handing out instructions." We're going to get annoyed at our kids or our spouses; we're going to mess up; our boundaries will become muddled at times — such is life. Sometimes we *will* be so busy we'll forget to take care of ourselves. Sometimes everything that can be scheduled *will* get scheduled for the same day. Will we remember at those times that life is a play? Will we still remember that parenting is a play?

We're going to get upset, but for how long? We're going to be anxious and afraid, but for how long? We're going to be busy, but for how long? Are we listening carefully to our bodies? Do we treat ourselves well? Do we love and respect our bodies and pay attention to our needs? Put the book down. Close your eyes and gently bring your attention to your breathing. Take however long you need to let yourself become still. Take as much time as you need to find the warm inner radiance that lies beneath all your surface thoughts and feelings. Once you find it, let yourself bask in it, revel in it, and know that we all share this same inner space. And even if you are unable to reach the inner radiance, keep trying. It is your very own treasure waiting to be discovered.

A Message from the Authors

Anne and Vic welcome correspondence. They can be reached by writing them

c/o The Essence of Parenting
P.O. Box 25
Lake Mills, WI 53551